CRUSH STRESS WHILE YOU WORK

Tips and Tricks To Stay Energized, Organized and Happy in Your Work Environment

Lolita Scesnaviciute Guarin

Copyright © 2017 Lolita Scesnaviciute Guarin
All rights reserved.

ISBN: 1542609798
ISBN 13: 9781542609791

This book was created for educational purposes only. The author disclaims all warranties with respect to the representation of the completeness of the contents and the accuracy of this book and should not be held liable for damages arising from it. The examples, advice, and explanations mentioned in this book might not be applicable and accurate in all situations. It should be applied depending on individual's mental and physical state.

CONTENTS

Introduction	ix
Relax Your Brain	1
Create a Morning Routine	2
Prepare the Night Before	3
Minimize Commitments	4
Single Tasks	5
Shut Off Your Inner Critic	6
Take Your Full Lunch Hour	7
Wear Headphones	8
Listen to Your Favorite Music	9
Count Backward	11
Watch a Funny Video	12
Write To Your Friend	13
Do a Crossword Puzzle	14
Coloring Books	15
Look Outside	16
Remember Doing What You Love	16
Remember a Great Vacation	17
Start Planning a Vacation	19
Be Grateful	20

Have a Special Place	21
Reward Yourself	22
Physical Activities That Reduce Stress	24
Breathe	25
Close Your Eyes	26
Take a Nap	27
Use a Stress Ball	28
Do Something Repetitive	28
Stretch Your Shoulders and Neck	29
Do Some Yoga	30
Take a Quick Walk	31
Run in Place	32
Get Yourself Comfortable	33
Stand at the Desk	34
Rub Your Feet	35
Exercise Your Hands	36
Dance	37
Do Something Very Slowly	38
Drip Cold Water on Your Wrists	39
Do Aromatherapy	40
Get in a Bubble	41
Exercise in the Morning	42
Do Nothing	43
10 Foods That Naturally Reduce Stress	44
Dark Chocolate	45
Avocado	45
Honey	46
Banana	47
Green tea	48
Oatmeal	48
Berries	49
Mango	50

Asparagus	50
Cashews	51
Coworkers	52
Listen to People	53
Build a Rapport	53
Have Manners	54
Be Respectful	55
Be Open-minded	56
See Greatness in Others	57
Change Your Point of View	58
Share Credit	59
Be Calm	59
Don't Assume	60
Stop the Bullying	61
Don't Point Fingers	62
Don't Blame	63
More Than Words	64
Clarify Your Intentions	65
Express Emotions	66
Apologize	67
Have the Last Word	68
Have an Escape Plan	68
5 Steps How to Deal With Negative People	70
How to Have a Difficult Conversation	74
Managing Your Time	77
Prioritize	78
Plan Your Day Ahead of Time	78
Use a Calendar	79
Time Your Activities	80
Intend To Be Early	81
Learn to Say "No"	82
Delegate	82

Single Task	83
Keep Small Stuff Small	84
Cut Short Long Conversations When You Need To	85
Love Your Workspace	86
Clean Your Workspace	86
Gather and Put It Back in its Place	87
Label Things	88
Improve Your Filing System	89
Clear Off Your Desk	89
Organize Your Drawers	90
Sort Mail	91
Assign Discard Dates	92
Bring Furniture to Work	92
Keep Yourself Inspired	93
About the Author	95

INTRODUCTION

"I don't have time for this!" exclaimed one of my clients; let's call her Mary. She threw her hands in the air. It was late Thursday evening when she attended her first stress management session with me. She wasn't happy to be there. She came to see me only because her family made her.

The previous week, Mary became very emotional, disoriented, and weak at her knees. She felt as if she would pass out, had shortness of breath, chest pain, and heart palpitations. All that landed her in the emergency room. Her family thought she had a heart attack – only to find out that it had to do with her stress levels, and she was having an anxiety attack. And the truth was, it wasn't the first time this had happened to her. Her family was afraid that it wasn't the last either.

Mary was a very hard working woman, but she wasn't a CEO of a big corporation or a manager of a large group of people. She was, however, responsible for a job with steep deadlines, constant overtime, never-ending demands from her boss and annoying coworkers. At home, she had a husband, two adorable kids. Oh, and a dog. So in comparison, Mary was a regular working mom who juggled responsibilities at work and home every day, like millions other of women all around the world.

I knew what she was going through. I remembered myself, five years before, collapsing on the kitchen floor just because my body couldn't take it anymore. Like Mary, I worked hard. I would get up very early, drive 25 miles to work to beat traffic, skipped lunches, worked extra hours to meet the deadlines, took care of my family as soon as I arrived home, and was the last to go to bed. That was my life, week after week, until it hit my body so hard that it knocked my hormones out of balance.

Hormones mean a lot to our bodies, as I came to learn. Our whole health depends on our hormones being balanced. I was exhausted, moody, tired, overweight, sleepless, and headachey. I was very irritable and angry and, just between us, I experienced serious feminine problems. After months of research for natural cures for stress, multiple workshops, and webinars on how to relax, change my diet, and start new exercise routines, I managed to bring myself back to health. I became so passionate about managing stress that I decided to help others by becoming a Certified Stress Management Coach to help others just like Mary.

"How do you expect me to go to work? Drive my kids to soccer practice, music rehearsals, cook, clean? And then somehow squeeze yoga and meditation into my day?" Mary argued against my suggestions. "There is no way for me to do that!" I could totally understand that she had no time to take a break and take care of herself. In today's fast-paced society, chased by the constant ticking of the clock, so many people feel guilty about just closing their eyes.

The truth is, nobody *has* time, right? But the key is to *make* time for things that are important to you. Just ask yourself, right now, what is most important in your life? If it's your family, then you have to take care of yourself because of your family. If you collapse, who will look after your family and the people you love? If you don't have enough energy for yourself, you can't give it to others. For Mary, I had to teach her to take care of herself, in the same way I had learned years before. Fortunately, she did come to understand my point that her health is more important than she thought. Mary then agreed to follow our daily Stress Management Plan. She built new healthy habits, and her anxiety attacks are a thing of the past.

So many of us spend the majority of our days at work and have to deal with circumstances that are out of our control. I decided to put this book together with the understanding that short tips and tricks can make a difference in your quality of life when dealing with workplace stress. By all means, I don't claim that this book alone can heal anxiety and stress entirely. Sometimes there are changes you need to make outside of your work environment. You might need to change your diet, and then I recommend getting advice from a nutritionist. You might need to integrate exercise under professional supervision. Whatever other supplemental steps you might need to take, this book is a good starting point in your journey to de-stress. The purpose of this book is to give you a guide to lower your stress levels while you work, so at the end of the day you still have energy left for your family and friends.

This book consists of 6 chapters on how to relax mentally and physically, how to deal with coworkers, what foods to eat to relax, and how to organize your space and time to save yourself from stress. I am not expecting you to take every single action in this book, but if you find some that are your favorites to improve your life even just a little, I will have accomplished my goal. No matter what reason you picked up this book, I wish you success. Yes, you can do it. Start with something small, don't give up on the process, and you will change your well-being.

RELAX YOUR BRAIN

I want to start this book with addressing mental productivity. The truth is, all ideas start in your brain. It doesn't matter if they are good or bad ideas, they all start with your brain power. Do you want to move mountains? You must take care of your brain – or your brain won't take care of you!

As Bob Proctor, leader in Prosperity and Personal Development states in his book, *You Were Born Rich*: "If you can see it in your mind, you're going to hold it in your hand." That is a scary thought! What if you're not able to see a dream or goal in your mind, because thinking hurts? What if you're so tired, overwhelmed, and exhausted mentally that just thinking of another task on your list makes you feel nauseous? What if, because of stress, you feel like getting into a car and driving away into the horizon without the intention of turning back?

But before you grab that steering wheel, take a breath and read on to learn simple tips and tricks that helped me and numerous friends and clients to find mental relief, before collapsing. I hope you will pencil them into your schedule and implement the ones that you find useful. Often.

Create a Morning Routine

Does it feel like time is just flying by? You woke up – it is Monday and the next morning – it is Friday already! Time flies because we keep on doing the same routine over and over. It might be boring for us, but surely routine is comfortable to our brain. The smoother the routine, the happier you will be. It's critical to plan how you'll start each morning. It makes an impact for the rest of your day! Mornings with routines are predictable and safe. Of course, there are many things that can disrupt the most planned morning. But you can be ready and organized so your day will start with as little stress as possible.

ACTIVITY: I recommend creating your perfect morning routine. Let's do an exercise together. We all have a morning routine. Think of yours. Are you happy with it? Is there something you could improve? Let's get started. 1. Think of all the things you do in the morning and write them down. 2. Once you have the list, group them by location in the house, so you can accomplish more without running around. 3. After you figure out what things you need to do, write them down in chronological order. 4. Follow your list of "to do's" in the morning to save you time and stress. You're welcome!

One of my friends used to be a mess in the mornings. First of all, she would wake up late and hit the snooze button as soon she would hear the alarm going off. I'm sure you know the feeling. After she was already late, she would get the kids ready for school in a hurry, which kept her in a stressed and angry state. Well, that didn't go well with her family relationships either. Her children saw their mother frustrated and overwhelmed all of the time. My friend would lash out at them for no reason and get stressed out over simple things. She knew she had to change.

After I recommended that she make a list, like the one described above, she became more organized. She arranged her activities by the area: bathroom, closet, kitchen. She delegated many things to her kids. And after a few days, they got into such a smooth routine, and the mornings became something to smile about. My friend became more organized, loving and peaceful in the process and her kids self-esteem improved too because their mother trusted them with the chores in the morning!

Prepare the Night Before
Are your mornings pleasant and relaxed? Do you have a routine down that keeps you confident for the rest of your day? Or is your morning a sequence of hurrying, running around, and trying to catch up with things that should have been taken care of yesterday? Is the example from the previous section about my friend familiar to you? If you do have a morning routine that works for you – great! If you don't, go back and re-read the step above and create your own routine.

I also recommend preparing many things the night before. Create your evening routine. There are plenty of things at night that you can do to make your mornings as pleasant as possible. And, I understand you are probably tired at night and don't want to do anything extra, but just remember how nice it will be to sleep longer because your morning is organized! Even ten minutes can make a difference. So, if you have an evening routine, you help yourself to be more organized and relaxed.

ACTIVITY: Make a list of your morning tasks that can be done the night before. This will save you so much time in the morning and keep you away from stress. These tasks might include: deciding what you will wear the night before; packing your lunch; gathering the things you will need in the morning, etc. What other things you can do the night before that will lighten your morning load? Include them into your evening routine.

In the mornings, I used to stand in the closet for fifteen minutes and wonder what I was going to wear that day. You know the feeling when you are staring at the full closet and think in horror to yourself, "There is nothing to wear!" Yep, that was my morning routine. When I worked in the corporate world, being late was a no-no, so this was a big problem for me. When I arranged my clothing the night before, dressing up became a pleasant morning experience. That's how easy it can be to turn the tables on stress once you've made your list and identified what you need to do the night before.

Minimize Commitments
We live in a never-ending to-do world. It takes time to keep a job and take care of the family. Many times, our friends, parents, neighbors, and coworkers need our help too.

ACTIVITY: It is important to be helpful, but it is critical not to obligate yourself to the point of overload where there is no time for yourself. You can't take care of everybody, especially in the workplace environment. Don't feel obligated to take on every job your supervisor or coworkers ask of you. If you already feel overwhelmed, you should communicate that to your supervisor. Trying to do everything that comes your way doesn't provide job security. Taking on too many tasks can prevent you from doing any of them well.

I had a coworker who took everything that got dropped on her desk. No matter the deadline, and no matter her current project load, she took on everything and anything. Every time somebody asked her for something, she would answer "Yes, I can do that!" She was afraid to tell her manager about being overwhelmed. She was afraid that if she said "No" to a project or task, she would get fired. Well, the opposite happened. She did so many things in a rush and in a stressed state that her quality of work diminished over time. At some point the mistakes were too big to forgive and management fired her.

Caring for the whole world is a noble thing. Unfortunately, it is also very stressful and energy depleting. Cut back on your commitments and try not to make more obligations that you know you can't fulfill. You can give to others when you have extra energy after taking care of yourself. But when you run on empty, there is nothing to offer.

Single Tasks
Everyone is very busy nowadays. There is an abundance of things that we need to do at work and at home, and it is hard to keep up. Multi-tasking can seem like the only way to accomplish things on time. Women are notorious multi-taskers. I envision a movie scene with a woman holding a baby in one hand, stirring a pot with the other, and talking on the phone at the same time. I know we have all been there!

It is well-documented that women are more capable of multi-tasking with greater results than men. I guess nature decided that there is no way to grow a family by single-tasking! But overall, who is multi-tasking is not that important. What is important is that the results are varying when someone is performing the same job multi-tasking, versus single-tasking. And if you are doing several things at the same time, the chances are some of them will get overlooked or be done poorly.

ACTIVITY: I don't recommend multi-tasking in the workplace. Performing many things at the same time can cost you stress and poor quality of work. It is an excellent idea to concentrate on one thing at a time and accomplish it with assurance than you did it well. And if someone asks you to multi-task, explain that your quality of work will suffer. I am sure they wouldn't want that! Mistakes take time and energy to fix. Why worry about that? Just do one task at a time and do it to the best of your ability. When you are done with one task, proceed to the next. Save yourself from stress and overload.

I had a friend who would stay extra hours after work and had to take work home over the weekend so he could fix the mistakes that he created while multi-tasking. He wasn't enjoying his work or doing it particularly well. He was complaining about his job and looking for a different workplace. He sought my help, so I pointed out that he needed to focus only on one thing at a time. He didn't like hearing that. But he listened, and after he started implementing my advice, he found that he made fewer errors, and he was able to enjoy his weekends again!

Shut Off Your Inner Critic
Every day we are bombarded by other people's opinions about us. We fear that maybe people are not telling us criticism to our face, but instead say what they really think about us behind our backs. Many times, we listen to criticism from our closest people, our family and friends, without filtering it. However, they are not always right! Some people just disagree for selfish reasons, and others will be insincere to keep you safe from taking a hard look at yourself or feeling negative circumstances. So, take all criticism and lack thereof with a dash of salt.

We could run away from other people and not listen to them. But there is a stronger voice that you can't escape from, and it lives between your two ears. Do you know who that is? It is your inner critic. Remember that voice in your head that keeps criticizing you? The one who tells you: "You shouldn't have!" when you hesitate; "Why did you do that again!?" when you fall into a familiar pattern; "You are not going to make it!" when you start something new; and worst of all, "You so stupid" when you make an honest mistake. Maybe your inner critic is not that harsh, but it still has something to say once in a while, and you need to be able to understand what it means. If you listen to your inner critic, then you start having self-doubts, you worry about things to come and next thing you know, you are stressed! The inner critic not only stresses you out but it also lowers your confidence and performance. Your inner critic's remarks are not just harmful to how you feel but also to your self-image.

ACTIVITY: Well, it is time to stop listening to your inner critic. The world around us is already stressing to us, why allow your inner thoughts to add to the pile? The inner critic is a survival mechanism; that's all. It is trying to protect you from being hurt. The next time your inner critic has a negative word, thank him for safe-guarding you and say "Thank you for sharing!" The more times you will proceed forward without listening to your inner critic, the more you will achieve. You will feel more confident and won't listen to your inner critic anymore. More than that, your inner critic will stop showing up!

There was a time when my inner critic would rule my life. No matter how small the task was, whenever I was doing something new and out of my comfort zone, she would try to talk me out of it. I was afraid to make phone calls or talk to people that I didn't know because my inner voice would point out my Lithuanian accent. I was reluctant to do anything new because my inner voice would remind me of my previous failures. Every person has an inner critic. But only successful people don't allow their inner critic to hold them back from what they want to do or who they want to be. And I can vouch for that one!

Take Your Full Lunch Hour
It is the cardinal rule to take a break and have lunch. Many workplaces even require that lunch be a full hour! Sure, we all want to go home sooner, and if there is a possibility to work through lunch, we all will take it at one time or another. If you are your own boss, then you might choose to work through lunch. Perhaps you are working through lunch because there is so much work to do, and eight hours a day is just not enough time to accomplish everything.

Whatever the case is for you, take the full hour lunch to relax and recharge. Of that hour, aim to take a break of at least 15-20 minutes. You will regret it if you won't. Without this break, your productivity will decrease, and your stress level will increase. Sometimes working through lunch is necessary, but try to relax. If you don't give yourself a break, who will? Sure, your boss loves your productivity, but he won't pay your health bills later. Take that hour to relax, do a physical activity, meditate, color that coloring book, eat or just chat with coworkers. You need it!

ACTIVITY: If you can, leave your workplace and go for lunch somewhere off site. It doesn't have to be a restaurant. You can bring your lunch and go outside the building or go to a nearby park. Leaving your immediate workplace relaxes your brain. You also can eat in one place and do exercises somewhere else. You could take a short power nap in the car during that break time! If you can't leave the office or choose to eat at your desk, you can still help yourself by practice mindful eating. It will look at first as if you are wasting your time just eating slowly. But later you will see significant benefits. Because when you are mindful even for 15 minutes a day, it keeps the stress away!

I used to eat my packed lunch with coworkers for half an hour and the other half I would go to for a walk or meditate in my car. Sometimes I could even take a short nap! At first, I had some coworkers rolling their eyes at me, but later I inspired them to join me for a walk outside and they were thankful for the stress relief. It just takes a little planning to make it happen!

Wear Headphones
Some people like noise around them while they work. That noise can be music, people chatting, radio or anything; there is a group of people that stays focused no matter what. But for some of us, noise can be tiring and even stressful when we are trying to work. This section is for the silence lovers.

If you are one of silence lovers, get yourself some headphones, and better yet - noise canceling headphones. Other people working around you can be very noisy. You are probably tired of listening to the same stories over and over again, or sometimes you are annoyed with that coworker that laughs so loudly that they could be heard across the street. Noise can be stressful. Also, it makes you tired faster.

ACTIVITY: Put the headphones on and forget about them! When you are wearing headphones, people will leave you alone. By wearing them you communicate to them that you are not available at the moment. Trust me, the people who truly need your attention, will tap you on a shoulder. You are trying to keep the time wasters at bay. And don't be afraid to hurt somebody's feelings. Explain to them, only if they ask, that silence helps you to concentrate and you perform your job better. I don't think anyone would object that. You can choose to sit with headphones on in silence or turn on the music you love. With headphones, it will be a superb experience!

I had a client who complained for months about the lack of silence in his office. His office wasn't very busy, but few very annoying employees would consistently talk for hours. And they sat right next to him in the office; he wouldn't escape them. His management didn't prevent them from gossiping every day, and it was disruptive to other employees. My recommendation to my client was to bring noise canceling headphones to work. And the next time the annoying coworkers started talking too long or too loudly, he put on his headphones. And what you think started to happen? The annoying coworkers took headphones as a sign that is time to leave! Everyone in the area was happier because my client did what he needed to do to take care of himself.

Listen to Your Favorite Music
Music, in the form of singing and chanting, has been used as self-expression by humans for a very long time. By now, nobody needs proof

that listening to music is very beneficial to us. There is the whole science about music vibrations and its positive influence on improving your mood but also improving your surroundings. Did you hear that cows that produce 7.5% more milk while listening to classical music? Or maybe you've heard that corn that grows faster and stronger and fuller while listening to music. It has been observed that sound vibrations destroyed the parasite microorganisms that harmed corn. Imagine what music can do for you!

Of course, these benefits depend on what kind of music you choose to listen to. It is proven that classical music emits more harmonious vibes than rock-and-roll. But you don't have to go for classical music if it is not your favorite! You are welcome to find the music that makes you feel good, calms and relaxes you, something that improves your mood. If there is a particular song that always uplifts you, then remember to play it when you are down! A song that lifts you up can also be something that you and your loved ones listen to. A song that reminds you of someone special, that puts a smile on your face.

ACTIVITY: Incorporate music into your work day and listen to it while you are at work. It relaxes your brain and you won't get so tired. If you are not sure what type of music you like, take time to find out. There are so many music videos on YouTube or Pandora radio stations that you can listen to it forever!

In one of my previous workplaces, there was a young engineer. He always listened to heavy rock with his headphones on. That was his way of keeping his brain energized. One day we had a fire alarm, and everybody evacuated the building except for him! Finally, a coworker saw him still sitting at his desk and rushed him out of there. Take this advice and do listen to music, but make sure you are still aware of your surroundings!

Count Backward

Have you tried counting imaginary sheep to fall asleep? I know I have! Did it work for you? It worked for me. And do you know why? Because counting calms our brains! In general, counting is an excellent way to relax. Or course, this only works if you pay attention to counting. If you think you are counting but still thinking of something that is stressing you out, then counting won't help. You have to dedicate yourself to it mindfully.

ACTIVITY: Take five minutes out of your day and just count to 50 and back. You will calm down – guaranteed!

Consider this: it is harder to fear an upcoming meeting with a boss, which preoccupies you, if you are preoccupied with remembering what number comes before forty-seven. If you try counting up and down and are still stressed, or counting becomes too easy, try counting in thousands and imagine writing numbers. Do you know a foreign language? Even better! Count backward in a foreign language. This should keep your mind occupied so soon your attention and reaction to stressful situations will change, making you calmer and more in control of your thoughts. This method works because you can't think negative and positive thoughts at the same time.

I used to have a coworker that was very stressed during the quarterly report season. My recommendation to her was to count in order to relax. She took my advice to give counting a try. She would count to one hundred loudly in her office. Even if she had the door shut, she would walk around and count with such an intonation, that it sounded as if she were arguing with somebody. The entire office would hear her. Some nicknamed her "Accountant," because of it. Maybe it looked awkward to us, but it worked for her!

Watch a Funny Video

If you are overwhelmed at work or just need to give your brain a break, watch a short funny video! Short funny videos can do magic! Everyone loves videos; they can switch our mood in a blink of an eye! That is why we love movies so much! And you don't have to wait until somebody shares a funny video, you can find it yourself. The internet is full of videos. With so many videos available on the internet these days it is hard to escape the craze. If you are a social media fan and use the apps to keep up with your friends, I am sure you can find somebody posting a funny video every day.

ACTIVITY: Find your favorite YouTube channel and visit regularly or subscribe to it. A short video of jumping cats afraid of spider will elevate your mood, no matter how low it is in the moment. On the other hand, if you don't like funny videos – watch something inspirational, such as inspirational speeches or a great empowerment story. The videos can be about business success, or how to be happy, or even religious inspiration. Pick something that works for you! Watch videos during your break at work on your own devices (Don't get in trouble for surfing on a work device!). Or course, not all videos are positive or are mood uplifting. I urge you to select those videos that make you smile and take you away from your stress.

There are some videos that I love so much that I've bookmarked them so that I can come back to them and watch them over and over. If I feel down or low in energy, I love watching videos of dogs and cats wearing boots for the first time! Have you seen it? If not, search for it and have a good laugh! I just can't stop laughing at how high they pick up their legs in the air. I can watch that and laugh over and over! At other times, if I need business inspiration and want to get fired up about my business, I watch inspirational videos by Tony Robbins, Les Brown, Jack Canfield, and the like. The kind of video that will lower my stress really depends on my mood. Find something that works for you!

Write To Your Friend

Do you sometimes feel stressed and have no one to talk to? Do you feel like you need to talk to your best friend and tell him or her how annoyed and stressed you are? It can be any stress: worry about an upcoming meeting, annoying coworker, or overwhelming upcoming deadline. Stop and think. Don't run around the office and talk to anyone who will listen about how hard your life is. They might not understand and some could gossip and spread the news for you. You don't want that. You need to vent without negative consequences.

I do not recommend calling a friend right there and then either. She could be busy. But there are other ways you can let the steam out! What would you like to tell your best friend if she was sitting in front of you? Imagine that she is and vent to her. If you have the opportunity to talk out loud in private – do that. One time, I was so upset at work that went to my car just to scream. After ten minutes of a passionate monolog I felt better. And guess what? I realized that the coworker whom I was upset with was smoking in their car a few spaces away from me. It was good that I wasn't mentioning any names! So I recommend first to make sure your privacy is safe before venting aloud.

ACTIVITY: If you don't have anywhere to talk privately, then write. Write it down on a piece of paper. You could keep a diary where you can write out your complaints. If you don't want to keep such a book or journal, (God forbid somebody will find it) then write on a piece of paper and throw it away after you feel better. If you don't feel like wasting paper, then you can type it out on a computer and then delete what you wrote.

So take five minutes and let go of everything that is stressing you out. You will feel better! It works magic for me. I have a notebook just for that. It is a small notebook, so I carry it in my purse and take it out when I need it. I capture my worries and stresses there and sometimes look back at what I wrote to see if there are patterns that I can address. It is not only a calming to me, but when I go back and read my thoughts, this also helps me to find my own solutions!

Do a Crossword Puzzle
The best way to relax your brain is to calm your thoughts. But, sometimes it is very hard to tell your brain just to stop thinking! If you find that to be the case, challenge your brain to work on something else; as long as the new topic does not focus on your worries because we want to keep your mind from regurgitating those thoughts. And I find that there is sometimes nothing better than a crossword puzzle to occupy your brain when you feel stress.

ACTIVITY: find a crossword puzzle in a newspaper from the break room (if your workplace provides one) or buy a crossword or Sudoku book or just print one out one from the internet. I can guarantee that after you take a break from work by occupying your brain with something different, you will feel the energy boost. Use your lunch break not just for eating and chatting with coworkers, but use it to energize your brain! You will lower stress levels and increase your productivity.

If you don't like crosswords, you are welcome to find other brain games that you will enjoy. Brain games that require concentration can help take your mind off whatever's worrying you. You can use a Rubik cube, brain teasers, riddles, puzzles and so on. Find something that works for you!

Once in a bookstore, I came across a book of medieval puzzles, riddles, enigmas, and conundrums. It was on sale, and I bought it thinking that it would be a great distraction to use during my day. My husband loves those kinds of stuff brain teasers and he started cracking those riddles as soon I showed him the book. That night he came to bed very late, after I was already sleeping. The next night the same thing happened, and the next. What can I say; our brain is such a natural problem solver. So be careful – puzzle solving can be addictive!

Coloring Books
Was it fun to color when you were a kid? How exciting was it to see the image appear on the paper? Remember how relaxing it was? Well, coloring books are back in fashion!

ACTIVITY: Even if you are an adult, you can adopt this great relaxing activity. If you find your thoughts from spinning around and can't calm your worries – grab a coloring book and occupy your brain with something that doesn't require straining your brain. It doesn't matter what colors you use; crayons, colored pencils, or markers. There are plenty of complicated coloring books for adults available in the bookstores, discount stores, and even grocery stores! You can even download images to color from the internet.

Coloring relaxes our brain because we are doing something repetitive and not complicated. We slip into that meditative state of mind that is so beneficial. Even 15 minutes a day will work miracles. Don't stress yourself over coloring! It should be a relaxing exercise for you and not be a chore! If you don't like the particular image - leave it. If you don't feel like finishing it at all – leave it. If you don't want to color today – don't!

Once I had a client who had trouble falling asleep, and she couldn't get a good night's rest. I recommended her to include coloring into her evening routine. I thought it would be very beneficial to do that before she went to sleep to calm her thoughts. The first week she loved the exercise and thanked me for the great advice. She would pull out her coloring book and enjoy the colors until she got sleepy. But one day, after few weeks of coaching, she told me "I can't do the coloring book anymore! It is so hard to keep myself awake to finish the image!" Naturally, I advised her to stop stressing herself out.

Look Outside

Take time during the day to look out the window. No matter how busy you are, schedule a break. Just looking at the sky will calm your nerves. Even if it is raining outside and you can't see the sun, it will be still beneficial. Online Newsletter "The Globe and Mail" in the article called "Better by design: How a hospital room can help patients heal" states that patients who had a window in their hospital rooms were healed twice as fast as those who did not have a window at all. Surprisingly, even printed pictures of nature helped patients recover faster! Imagine what looking outside can do for you!

ACTIVITY: If your workspace is next to windows, take the time to look out. If your desk faces a window, turn that chair around and stare outside once in a while during the day. If you are not close to a window, make an effort to find one when you can. Maybe there is a window in the break room. Take a look. Stop by the window every time you go for a drink. If there is an opportunity, eat your lunch outside. You can also have an image on your desk or on your computer screen that you can look often. Pick a picture that you find inspiring and calming. It can be something that you find on the internet of a destination where you would love to go. It can be a picture of your family from your last vacation in Cancun. Or just a calming nature image that guides your mind to wander.

A few semesters in college I worked as an intern. I was seated by my mentor in his corner office. Not many people wanted to sit there close to the boss, but my desk faced downtown, and the panoramic view of about 200 degrees left and right. I saw the rain come and go. I saw the leaves on the trees changing throughout the year. I can't tell how much I loved that workplace! I was sad to leave.

Remember Doing What You Love

Is there an activity that you love doing? It can be cooking, knitting, mountain climbing, visiting your friends, or watching you favorite show on TV! I am not recommending doing these things during your work hours, but I am urging you to think about doing them. Seriously, the brain doesn't know when you are thinking about something or when it is happening for real. Let's reap the benefits!

ACTIVITY: Take few minutes to relax, close your eyes and remember how it feels to do what you love doing it! If you love to hang out with your friends, remember the last time you got together with them, remember what you did. Who was there? What did you talk about? Did you eat something? What did it taste like? Did you enjoy the place? Do you love scrapbooking? What is your favorite color? How often do you scrapbook? Do you belong to a group that does that together? Is there another meeting planned already? If not, plan another time when you will scrapbook, chat with friends or climb a mountain. It's up to you.

Did you remember something you love to do? Did you notice that you felt better as soon you started thinking of it? Did it place a smile on your face? Good! Now, I want you to remember doing the thing you love every day, at any free moment you get and not only in a workplace.

For example, I love cooking. I take a few minutes a day to browse the internet for new delicious and healthy recipes. I imagine cooking it, putting in on the plates, and arranging the dinner table. I even imagine how much my family will enjoy it! That always makes me smile and gives an extra energy boost to look forward to dinner.

Remember a Great Vacation
Are you stressed? Do you feel like going on vacation? Do you wish you could travel, but you can't get away at the moment? Was there a vacation in the past that you went on, and it made you feel great? Now is time to remember the details! The trick is in the brain: it doesn't

know when things are happening for real or are just make believe. A great memory will take you back to your amazing trip!

ACTIVITY: Close your eyes for a minute and remember how wonderful it was. Where did you go? What did you do? What did you eat? Who were you with? What were you wearing? Was it hot or cold? Remember all the details as much as you can and remember how you felt. If you do remember a great vacation and have pictures, make them a screen saver on your cell phone or computer, frame some for your desk, or keep them in your wallet, anywhere where you can easily gaze at them. Do you have a video on your phone? Even better! When you can recall your memory by looking at the images or listening to the sounds from the past and make yourself happy for the moment!

If you have a memory of a great vacation that you took with someone you love, but who is no longer with you, don't be sad or miss them. The point is to remember the happy moments, making yourself feel and to think positive thoughts. I am positive your loved one would like you to be happy and relaxed! Take few minutes to remember that comfortable, free feeling every day and watch your stress melt away!

I recommend remembering happy vacations because the point of this exercise is to relax, not to get stressed. I had a client who I suggested the same visualizing exercise, but after she dug into her memory, she couldn't find one nice vacation that she would want to remember! Her childhood holidays were filled with screaming, bullying, and fighting with her brothers. When she was married, she argued and struggled with her ex-husband about everything. With no happy vacation memory to recall, my recommendation to her was to imagine a perfect vacation! As I said – brain doesn't know if what you are thinking about is real or make believe. As long as it makes you feel great!

Start Planning a Vacation
Take time to plan your perfect vacation. Take a break from the overwhelming day by planning your next destination to enjoy, even if it is months away, or even just plan as a way to daydream. Browse the internet for some great travel destinations and look at the pictures. If you like looking at magazines, take the time to visit a bookstore for a few hours and browse for amazing places to explore. You see, the brain doesn't know when things are happening in reality and when it is not. Just thinking of something relaxing and seeing the images will give you a boost of energy and pick your mood up.

ACTIVITY: Imagine yourself lying on the beach, feel the sun kissing your skin, hear the seagulls close by. Did that make you feel good? If your relaxation choice includes more museum hall visits than visiting the beach, check out some great museums online that you would love to visit. Or maybe you like mountain climbing and camping, then plan that! Find something that makes you smile.

Don't think about money; imagine you have all the money and time in the world. You can even pretend to purchase a vacation package, go all the way through the purchase process, just don't push "submit order." Try making it as real as possible for yourself. Imagine who will you go with? You even can involve your friends or significant other in the process.

I had a friend who was playing this game and was looking for the perfect vacation that included a golfing experience. She looked at so many magazines and online websites that she could tell me the locations of all of the best golf courses. Her husband also happened to be a big golfer and a month before his birthday, he said to my friend "Let's go easy on that gift, honey". He was a little disappointed to find out that the perfect golf vacation was just a stress relief game!

Luckily, they were still able to purchase the vacation package and they had the best time of their lives.

Be Grateful

What are your first thoughts upon waking up? Are they positive or negative? For many of us, the first thing that we remember is something from the day before. Hopefully something that happened yesterday makes us feel good, but what if yesterday's memories bring us sadness or anger? The mood that you plug into first thing in the morning can influence your mood, productivity, and success rate for the rest of the day. I am sure you want to keep your positivity ratings high.

There is a way to turn any negative feelings into positive ones. And no matter if it is early morning or in the middle of the day. Practice being grateful! It is already proven many times that gratitude makes miracles. The secret is that when you think positive thoughts, you are not thinking negatively! You just can't think two thoughts at the same time! You can't feel positive and negative emotions at the same time. And the more you concentrate on positive thoughts, the more you will see the positive in your life.

ACTIVITY: Every morning write down at least ten things that you are grateful for in your life. It can be something small or big, as long you are feeling grateful when you writing it down. If you don't want to write it down, then think of it while you prepare yourself for the day. Count your blessings anytime you have a free moment and your day will go by more smoothly and stress free!

My mornings used to be very negative because I would relive the memory of yesterday's failures, sadness, or anger. Let me tell you, I didn't like my mornings much. I would replay failures from yesterday in my mind, start regretting them, planning my revenge, remembering something else negative from many years ago that didn't even matter today, and that would make me angry.

And one day I decided to take that time to be grateful for what I had and who I was. And my days changed! As soon I woke up, I started naming all the great things I have in my life: being able to walk, talk, my good health, having a loving family, having my parents close by, having a roof over my head, living in a nice home, and more. You don't have to be a millionaire to have things you are grateful for. Find those little things that make you smile and appreciate them!

Have a Special Place
Sometimes there are moments during the day when you feel like just running away from everything. I recommend that you got to your special place as soon you feel that way. Take a short break, close your eyes, and leave your worries behind, even if just for five minutes. More than that, I recommend you running away every day for at least a few minutes.

Of course, I don't recommend running away in reality, but in your mind! Have a place in your mind where you can relax when you feel overwhelmed and stressed out. What special place in this world makes you feel relaxed and confident? If you don't have a place in real life, imagine one! Your special place can be on the beach, in the backyard, on the mountain, or in a beautiful house. You are the one who chooses it, as long as it relaxes you.

ACTIVITY: Imagine specific details. How does the place look? How does it smell? What sounds can you hear? Who is with you? Not sure what kind of place to imagine? Take time to browse the internet or look through travel magazines in the bookstore (probably outside of your work hours). There are so many great inspirational and relaxing places in the world to choose from!

My run away place is a beautiful sunny open space house on a white sandy beach. All the big windows are open in the house. White light drapes move with the wind... I feel the light warm breeze blowing through in and touching my face... I can smell the flowers outside and hear the seagulls in the distance. I am sitting on a comfortable sofa, and my dog is by my side, his head on my lap, and I am happily patting him.

Ah....that felt good! Now it is your turn!

Reward Yourself
Many people have a problem with rewarding themselves. They think they are not worthy or not good enough to receive something or to be acknowledged. Receiving something positive has a stigma of being selfishness in our society. However, rewards are not as bad as you may think. They are extremely important in our lives! Could you imagine sports without any rewards? Getting paid for the job you do is also a reward. You know the feeling when you have accomplished something, such as: meeting an important deadline, finishing that big report or finally cleaning your office? You feel so proud of yourself, even if it is not a big deal to others? Well, reward yourself! Pat yourself on the shoulder! If you don't do that, who else will acknowledge you?

ACTIVITY: Before you start a new day, create a new to-do list or project list. Determine how you will reward yourself for each completed accomplishment. Think of something that you love to do and treat yourself to a spa or that special muffin you love or a pair of new shoes. When you know that there is a reward at the end, you won't dread doing the work. You will actually look forward to it!

I had a client that was suffering from low self-esteem and feeling unworthy of success. He was telling himself over and over that he can't accomplish things. I told him to write a to-do list, and after every task was completed to cross it off. More than that, I told him at the beginning of the day to think of a way he would reward himself after he finished his to-do list. After few weeks, his performance and self-confidence increased because he proved to himself that he could achieve things. More than that, every morning he was looking forward to going to work. At the end of the day he could enjoy his rewards.

PHYSICAL ACTIVITIES THAT REDUCE STRESS

I am sure you know the feeling: working on something so intensely that don't notice how a few hours just passed by! Your knees hurt, your hands are stiff, and you can't feel your buttocks anymore. Also, your neck is stiff from being all tucked in into your shoulders, and your eyes hurting like hell. I used to work so much that only my bladder would make me get up from my desk. Getting up and moving around looked to me as a major waste of time. Doing a small physical activity didn't make sense to me. I couldn't believe that having short breaks all throughout the day would make any difference.

Sadly, I was not only one living in disbelief. Government statistics show a gloomy reality that half of the people sit more than six hours a day. James Levine, co-director of Obesity Solutions at Mayo Clinic says "If you've been sitting for an hour, you've been sitting too long." Sedimentary lifestyles have been proven to lead to cardiovascular diseases, high blood pressure, colon cancer, diabetes, osteoporosis, anxiety, and depression.

If you are hitting the gym before or after work, doing yoga or Pilates, congratulate yourself. But do you move a lot during the day? If not, below are few ideas of how you can relax physically in a short time without disrupting your busy day and still reap the benefits of simply movement.

Breathe
It is amazing that something like breathing can make a huge difference to your wellbeing. We underestimate the influence of actions that we do every day. Just because of everyone breathes, this doesn't mean that breathing is that simple! I know – such an easy thing as breathing can actually help to lower stress if you do it right!

First of all, many people breathe shallow or even have a tendency to hold their breath when they are stressed. That deprives the brain of oxygen! I used to be guilty of that problem. I would have to remind myself to breathe in and out when I was stressed. Thankfully I learned a few techniques on how to breathe during tough moments. It became a habit and I will share it with you.

ACTIVITY: So, if you are stressed or worried or just not feeling well, try breathing in and out deeply and very slowly ten times. When you do deep breathing, your heart rate and brain waves slows down, your blood pressure falls, and you start feeling much better. Try breathing in deeply and breathing out loudly with your voice by saying "Ahhhh…..". Get everything out. Relax. While breathing out, listen to the sound of your voice, tune everything else out and go as long as you need to, until you run out of breath.

You can also try pranayama breathing, a yogic method that involves breathing through one nostril at a time. The technique is supposed to work the same way as acupuncture, by balancing your mind and body, to relieve stress and anxiety.

I had a client who would get very nervous before giving a presentation. She would get so nervous that she would become nauseous! My recommendation to her was to breathe in and out by counting to ten before every presentation. It worked well for her because by concentrating on slow breathing, she took her attention away from something that scared her. At the same time, the slow breathing slowed her heart rate and gave her plenty of oxygen to her brain to be great in presentation!

Close Your Eyes
Closing your eyes once in a while is ok! We are so busy that closing our eyes sounds as a waste of time. However, we need to pencil this activity into our schedule. Closing your eyes lowers your stress level by disconnecting from your surroundings and gives your eyes a quick rest. I understand, when there is so much to do through the day it is hard to find a spare minute, but seriously – you can manage that! It might seem like a lot of time, one minute here or there, but in reality, it's just a moment. Rub your eyes gently with a finger, to massage your eyeballs. It will make a difference.

ACTIVITY: Take a risk in looking funny to others and close your eyes. Don't be afraid of coworkers asking "Is everything ok with you?" Just answer them "I'm just resting my eyes, you should try it!" Try closing your eyes as often as you can. If you have a document loading on the screen – close your eyes! If you are taking a restroom break – close your eyes. While waiting for your coffee to fill your cup - close your eyes for few seconds.

I had a client who would work hard long hours. Being "mompreneur" she had to do a lot of things by herself. She claimed her eyes hurt so much at the end of the day that her vision would get blurry. That wasn't a good sign! My recommendation to her was to close her eyes while she talks on the phone. Since she talks so much on the phone and can't do anything else during that time, closing her eyes helped her to relax and concentrating on the person that she was conversing with helped her find relaxation.

Take a Nap

There is nothing better in combating stress than taking a nap! Naps improve productivity and wellbeing. I know - you are probably thinking, how in the world you can take a nap in the middle of the day! Well, you have a lunch break, right? If you don't take a lunch break now, here is a reason to make it happen! Take a 20-minute break to take a nap or to meditate.

ACTIVITY: Have a small pillow around for a quick power nap. It is possible to nap during the day – with a little planning! Use your break during the day to lay your head down for a few minutes. You can use an empty conference room or just your desk to relax. When you finally relax on that pillow, and I hope you find a place to do it, imagine that it is a sponge sucking up all your stress and worries. Just make sure you put an alarm on your phone to wake you up when time is up.

Find a place to nap can be tricky. If you have the luxury of having your own office – close the door for a power nap. Although not everyone has offices anymore, (usually only management), remember, meeting rooms can be used for everyone. Find an empty conference room, first check to make sure you are not taking the space for a meeting and take a nap. If you don't have the possibility for privacy – use your car. Park far away from the building, in a corner where you won't be disturbed.

Once I had a coworker who would take a nap every day. He would grab a briefcase and head towards the conference room. His times would vary, but most of his "meetings" were during the lunch hour. A few coworkers thought that he is running a business on the side. As it turns out, he was just taking naps during his lunch break and used his briefcase as a pillow! Someone discovered him snoring in one of the conference rooms, but that was okay. For Christmas, we surprised him with a real pillow.

Use a Stress Ball

Have you heard of stress balls? Do you have some? If not, find a few to keep on hand! There are two types of stress balls: hard and soft balls. Baoding balls were invented during the Ming Dynasty (1368-1644) in Baoding, China. Originally made of iron, they also can be made of wood. Usually, they are solid, but if you come across the hollowed out ones with chimes inside, get those. It is believed that the chimes inside the ball help balance energies. Overall, stress balls work by stimulating acupressure points in your hand and benefiting the whole body.

Find something that works for you. If you don't like stress balls, it doesn't have to be a ball. It can be something squeezable, no matter what shape or size. Don't like the noise? Get something quiet. If you don't want to buy anything? Look around your office or workplace. Companies usually have plenty of promotional rubber items that you can squeeze for free.

ACTIVITY: On days when you want to strangle a coworker, your partner, or the driver in the car in front of you, squeeze or roll stress balls instead. This is an easy, non-violent, and cheap way to ease the tension. Redirecting your attention on something else when you are upset can be a miracle.

For example, I just love to squeeze a chicken pet squeaky toy. It always makes me laugh! I used to go to the sports store and squeeze as many as I could and let them go all at once. That sad choir could be heard throughout the whole store! I would run to the other aisle and watch people's reactions. A few years ago, my husband gave me one for Christmas; now I have a collection! I can squeeze them anytime I want! Like right now! Yes, I just did it!

Do Something Repetitive

There is evidence that repetitive motion such as filing paperwork, brushing hair, or even swiveling in a chair can cause the body to relax. Repetitive actions calm the brain. That is why the brain loves routine so much! I think it happens because we are doing something that we have done so many times that we are more than confident about the outcome. My brain relaxes so much when I drive home that sometimes I don't remember how I got there! Leaving the house and going somewhere feels like it takes more time than my return home trip! Does that happen to you?

ACTIVITY: Find some repetitive action that helps you to relax. It would be great if you can find something that you would do for work anyway. Maybe there are files for you to file, delete some entries, or organize some boxes. It can be something as simple as swinging your leg for few minutes. Make a list of those activities, including all the things that you do that are constantly repeating. Read that list when you feel stressed. Go down the list and do something that both is useful at the moment and will also relax you!

A word of caution - don't write down anything that you have to do repetitively when you are in a hurry. That is stressing you out and not helping you to relax at all. The same counts for a work environment where you have to perform something repetitively all day long. In this case, you just need to take a break and do another activity in this book.

Stretch Your Shoulders and Neck
We all know how good it feels to stretch. When was the last time you took a nice stretch? Taking time for a quick stretch can relieve muscle tension and helps you to relax anytime, not only during a stressful day. This activity is such a thing that you can do in any workspace. Maybe stretching is not for an astronaut in his spacesuit, but for the rest of us, it is very doable.

ACTIVITY: Stretch your neck by dropping your right ear toward your right shoulder without lifting your right shoulder. With your right hand pull your head down to apply pressure on your head to help you to stretch the neck muscles deeper. Hold for a few seconds. Change sides. Then roll your shoulders around, forward and back, lift both shoulders up to the ears and drop them down. Repeat these exercises a few times while breathing. The key to proper stretching is to relax, breathe freely, do it very slowly, and hold the stretch for at least 30 seconds. Don't bounce or stretch when it is painful; you could injure yourself. Be easy on your body! You should enjoy it. You can stretch while on the phone, while waiting for your cup of tea or coffee to brew, or while waiting for your document to print.

And seriously, it doesn't take much time to steal a quick stretch throughout of your day. I used to have a coworker who would stretch any chance she got. It was a little weird at first. While we talked, she would start rolling her head around, but I got used to it. Later on, we would both stretch our necks while we carried on a conversation!

Do Some Yoga
To reduce stress and relax during your day do some yoga poses! I know, I know – you probably read that and made a funny facial expression. Yes, you could go to a yoga class during your lunch break or in the evening after work. But there are plenty of simple yoga poses that you can do anywhere you are.

You are probably questioning why I am differentiating between yoga and just stretching. Well, yoga is more about deep breathing, mindfulness, and balance in the whole body. And stretching your neck could be done in few seconds while standing in line for your lunch. Performing simple yoga moves while you are busy is easier than you think. Here are a few poses that I would like to share with you that usually work magic for me. So I hope you will like them, too!

ACTIVITY: While sitting on your chair, straighten your spine. Take a deep breath and hold it for few seconds. Then stretch your hands all the way up to the ceiling like you are trying to reach something located very high. Hold for few seconds, then put your arms down, and breathe out.

While seated, twist to one side from the bottom of your spine grabbing your armrest, like you are trying to reach something that is behind you. Hold for a few seconds, release, and repeat as many times as you feel like.

Stand a few feet from your desk and put of your both hands on the top of the desk. Drop your head between your arms, stretch, and relax for few seconds. Yes, it will make your butt stick out, but the exercise is well worth the try!

While standing, soften your knees, fold over in half and let your body rest. Let your head and hands to dangle freely. Hold the posture for at least 20 seconds and sway your hands from side to side. There – you see, very simple yoga exercises, you can do! It is not that difficult!

If there is a room that you can use undisturbed, and if you feel comfortable, lie down on the ground, take your shoes off, and put your feet up against the wall. Close your eyes, rest as much as you can. Just make sure you put an alarm on your phone to wake you up. To be awakened by the coworkers assembling for a meeting is not fun (I experienced this first hand)!

Take a Quick Walk
The Sunwarrior website states that a 30-minute walk every day is a great antidepressant. While you walk, your body releases feel-good endorphins, which reduce stress and anxiety. Walking not only elevates your mood, but it also helps you to fight dementia, fatigue, inadequate sleep, heart disease, and many kinds of cancer.

But why wait until you come home from work to walk? Use every moment you get during your work day. I would not recommend walking outside if the weather conditions would make you feel sick, unsafe or uncomfortable. Walking should be a stress-less experience.

ACTIVITY: When you're feeling overwhelmed, having trouble concentrating, or somebody is making your life miserable, and you just need to get out for a second, take a quick walk around the block. You will be alone to sort out your thoughts. Or you can invite a companion to walk with if you feel like having company. If you don't have the possibility to get out in the open, then take a walk around your workspace. If you are going to a meeting, retrieving something from the printer, or for a cup of water, take the longest route to get there. Even if there is no reason at all to walk around – just take a break and do it!

I used to have a coworker, who was an older man, and throughout the days he was walking back and forward to me, always with a handful of papers. We wondered why he is so busy moving around. One day, some coworkers and I followed him. Yes, I know, childish, but I wouldn't resist making my day more exciting. And guess where he was going? Nowhere! He was just walking in circles! It was good for him. If you ask me about his health, when I think of it, he was a healthy, funny guy.

Run in Place
If you feel stressed, tired, or sleepy, take a run! Running, overall, is a great practice to improve your health and combat stress. *Runner's World* states that running makes you healthier, strengthens your bones, helps with your mental health, and makes you happier. Word of caution: wear comfortable shoes and warm up first if you are planning on a fast run. I don't recommend running around the office since you can injure not only yourself but also others on your way. I don't recommend running in circles either. You could get dizzy or become nauseous.

ACTIVITY: If you can't run outside, around the block or hit the gym anytime you want, run in place. Even if you are at your desk in your office or cubicle. Just stand up and run in place for a few minutes. Run as long as you want, as fast as you want! Get those endorphins going through your whole body.

I used to run in place while my tea cup filled up. I would do a short fasted power run. It would get my blood flowing making me more alert. I also would feel proud of myself since I did something to help myself to feel better! So I recommend you do the same. It takes very little time, but it will help you stay energized all day.

Get Yourself Comfortable
It is surprising how much energy we waste on feeling uncomfortable. If something is bothering you, no matter how small it is, over time, it can make you feel tired and angry.

ACTIVITY: If you feel suddenly out of balance and don't know why you are irritated, ask yourself, "Do I feel comfortable?" Review the possible sources of discomfort that I listed for you to find what's making you uncomfortable and change it!

1. If you are sitting at your desk, make sure you are sitting in a comfortable chair. Attempt to sit with your back straight and do not slouch. If the chair doesn't give you comfort, find another one. Ask your workplace administrator to provide more comfortable seating arrangements. I know, I know, they probably won't care. But at least you asked! And who knows, perhaps you will get a better chair, or be allowed to bring your own.

2. Wear comfortable clothing. Clothing that is too tight or too big will make you feel uncomfortable. You will get tired faster not only because you are wearing uncomfortable clothing, but also deep

down you feel uncomfortable mentally. If you don't feel good about yourself, you will feel stress.

3. Wear comfortable shoes. If you just must have those high heels, that is fine, but have a pair of back-up shoes under your desk to lessen your stress. If you stand all day, then comfortable shoes are a life-saver. If you stand in one place a lot, then invest in a standing mat.

4. Keep yourself at a perfect temperature. If you feel cold - have a sweater, heater or a blanket to warm you up. If you are hot – get a fan! If your work environment is regulated by the air conditioner, ask your coworkers in the area around you if they are uncomfortable, too. Maybe you are not the only one in the workplace suffering. Find out who is responsible for the temperature and ask for help.

5. Keep yourself hydrated and fed. So many times we can get cranky like a three-year-old toddler just because we are hungry or thirsty. Take good care of yourself!

My friend gave me bunny slippers for Christmas and I just felt in love with them. They keep my feet not only super comfortable, but also warm! And the best part – I would get a smile from anybody who saw me wear them around the office.

Stand at the Desk
Depending on your work environment, you may sit for long periods at a time. Hopefully, you don't sit all day long. It has been proven that all day sitting and not moving is very harmful to our bodies. Sitting all day long contributes to obesity which is associated with high blood sugar, increased blood pressure, and increased cholesterol levels. Too much sitting a day also produces the risk of cardiovascular disease and colon cancer. In addition, I don't think there are enough endorphins to generate a good mood while you sit all day. Even if you are

having a winning hand in Las Vegas, but have been sitting all day long, you still need to stand up!

ACTIVITY: Get off that chair as often as possible. Period.

If you can't leave your workspace, just stand up. If you conduct business from home, get an adjustable standing desk. If you work for a company, request one. Adjustable desks are very popular. And as with anything new, everyone has an opinion about it. Some supporter's feedback says that it is a good idea to stand all day. While some opposing views say that it is not a good idea to stand all day, only 20 minutes an hour should be enough.

My take on this subject – stand as much as you want, but don't stress yourself over it. The activity should help you to relax, not make you tired. Personally, I can't stand more than 20 minutes an hour at my desk. My back starts hurting if I stand more than that. I have a client who works all day at the desk, standing and walking on the treadmill. It works for him. Find a way that works for you. If you can't stand at the desk for a longer time, at least stand-up and walk around. Just move as much as you can.

Rub Your Feet
If you stand all day, or if you walk a lot, the circulation in the feet is disrupted. Foot massage is very relaxing and healthy even if you sit all day. Foot massage is proven not only to increase blood flow to your legs, but also to lower stress and anxiety levels, headaches and migraines, and blood lowers pressure. Having a 10 to 20-minute foot massage three times a week or more often can work miracles for your health. At any chance you get, rub your feet. It would be great if you have the luxury of getting a foot massage from a professional. But you could massage your feet yourself during any break you get at work or at home. I like rubbing my feet while I am watching TV or talking on the phone.

ACTIVITY: Massage your feet in circular motions. Start with your toes, move to the arch of your foot and then the heel. You also can achieve great results if you use a tennis or golf ball. This technique is a great alternative if you don't want to touch your feet with your hands or massage your feet while you are busy with something else. Put the ball on the floor and rub your feet by rolling the ball under your foot.

There are other great exercises especially if you don't want to tire your hands by rubbing your feet or if you don't have any tennis or golf balls on hand. Lift one foot and point toward the ground, flex your foot. Squeeze your toes as if you were making a claw, then hold for a few seconds. Let go and relax.

Exercise Your Hands
It is nice to have a foot massage, but don't forget about the other parts of your body that get fatigued– like your hands. If you use hands for typing or any other repetitive work that keeps your wrists stagnant for most of the day, you need to use exercises to keep them healthy. Simple exercises repeated a few times a day would release the pressure and tension for tired, over used hands. Even if your hands are not tired, any relaxing movement will benefit you.

ACTIVITY: Clasp your hands together and roll them around, in both directions. Then, relax your wrists and move your clasped hands around, with your wrists being loose. Continue for 30 seconds. After that, let your hands rest and shake them.

Another good exercise, especially for those who sit at the desk all day, is to sit or stand straight and relax your shoulders. Fully extend your hands, palms facing forward. Pull your fingers back towards yourself with your arm by pressuring with the opposite hand. Wait 5-10 seconds. Make a fist and curve your wrist down, pressure with the opposite hand.

Simple hand exercises don't take much of your time. There is no excuse not to take a minute during the day to relax your hands. Do these exercises a couple of times every hour! It will help not only your hands, but also it will also give your mind a break. You are welcome to close your eyes and breathe deeply while you are doing your hand exercises. Better yet, while you are at it, massage every finger and apply pressure to acupuncture points to get the full benefits of stress relief. Why not use the moment entirely!? I exercise my hands every hour for a few seconds. That's a habit that I built by adding to my one-minute mindfulness break. It works for me!

Dance
We don't need a research to prove that dancing to your favorite song reduces stress. I am sure this is not news to you! It is a great idea to incorporate dance into your day. Dancing not only helps your body to relax, but it also improves brain function and memory. When you dance, your heart, lungs, muscles and bones benefit and get stronger! You also gain better flexibility and balance. Did you know that we love music as soon as we are born? Infants as young as two months old already respond to music! Have you seen children respond to music? As soon they hear music they love – they dance! They move their bodies! And look at them all happy!

ACTIVITY: Taking a quick break? Dance a little. Waiting for that cup of coffee to fill up? Dance! I heard there are some companies that start work day by putting on joyful music and let their employees dance. That is an excellent way to start the day! Listen to music that you love – move that body! Do you have some special moves that can put you in a better mood? Use them anytime you have a moment!

Friedrich Nietzsche, a famous 19th century philosopher, once said, "We should consider every day lost on which we have not danced at least once." And I agree with him. It doesn't take that much time to steal a dance or two out of your busy day. You don't have to sweat to it, just a few minutes while you are taking a break will put a smile on your face and relax your body and brain! Remember the last time you danced, and it was fun, right? Even if that was ten years ago, it still could be fun right now. Listen to music that you love – move that body! Do you have some special moves that can put you in a better mood? Use them anytime you have a moment.

Do Something Very Slowly
There are multiple ways to relax. Meditation is one of the wonderful ways you can relax your body and mind. But what if you can't meditate? How can you get to the point of relaxation? It is proven that doing something extra slowly relaxes the brain and works as meditation. By doing something very slowly, your brain concentrates on the action and releases many thoughts that keep running in your head.

ACTIVITY: You should take a break and do something very slowly. You can take a walk. Which may not seem like meditation at all, but if you walk very slowly, extremely slowly, you will understand what I am talking about. You can even read a book or write a note but write every letter as if you were about to fall asleep. You can clean or organize something slowly as well. Although, I don't recommend driving your car very slowly, or fellow drivers would be upset.

This activity will probably take more than five minutes to be effective. The longer you do it, the better the results. I do not recommend you do something slowly if you are on a pressing deadline. If you want to practice a slow relaxation method, put it on your daily to-do list. Schedule an appointment with yourself during the busy day to relax that way. You have to let yourself relax. Or it will never happen on its own.

One of my clients was working as an office administrator. She was very busy during the day and had one of those never-ending to-do lists. My recommendation to her was to slow down and take a break. She would try her best. One day she decided to try the slow movement method to relax. She was organizing folders on her desk so slowly, that her supervisor asked her to come in for a chat. He asked her if everything ok and if she felt appreciated in her work environment. After a short explanation of her new relaxation method, they had a good laugh!

Drip Cold Water on Your Wrists
When I first heard about cold water being an excellent way to de-stress, the first image that came to my mind was of an upset person being plunged into a barrel of cold water. You can imagine the poor man's expression on his face! But seriously, cold water helps the body to relax.

ACTIVITY: When you get stressed, go into a bathroom and let the cold water run down your hands and wash your face. It is also a good idea to drop some cold water behind your earlobes. These are two spots on the body with major arteries that are located right underneath the skin, so cooling these areas can help you to calm the whole body. I think this is an especially good exercise because by going into the bathroom you also removed yourself from the stressful situation and redirected your attention. While you are letting that water run, close your eyes and breathe in deeply a few times. If you are actually cold, then cold water won't help you. In this case, comfort yourself by emerging your hands in warm water.

I had a coworker who would take a break when stressed by applying cold water to her hands as well as to her face. Before she would go to the lady's room, she would tell me "Going to take a cold shower!" You can use this great technique not only to calm yourself but also to gain clarity and focus.

Do Aromatherapy

It is not a secret that aromatherapy is one of the great tools to battle stress. It is also severely overlooked and considered useless by many skeptics. Don't underestimate the power of aromas! Aromatherapy has been around for centuries and has been shown to relax the brain, decrease stress levels and make your state of mind happy.

Take a second to inhale the aroma of relaxing essential oils. Many grocery stores have essential oils in the mind and body care sections so you can choose something inexpensive. Others prefer to have aromatherapy candles. There are essential oil companies that sell pendants you can place a drop of oil, and the relaxing smell will keep you company all day long. But depending on your workspace, some people around you may not like the constant smell, no matter how pleasant it is.

You can choose to experience aromatherapy in a way that works best for you, and then chose scents that appeal to you. Here are some scents that will relieve your stress: lavender oil, valerian root, patchouli, chamomile, sage, eucalyptus, basil, peppermint, and others. You can also use premade essential oil mixes that are labeled "Stress Release" or "Relax."

ACTIVITY: You can sniff essential oil directly from the bottle while taking in deep inhalations. Or wet the cotton ball with the oil and sniff it 3-4 times a day.

I keep at least three bottles of essential oils on my desk. I used to remind myself to sniff when I talked on the phone or during one of my breaks. I just closed my eyes and relaxed. By now, I just grab one of them and sniff without thinking about it. It became a habit and I like it. It makes me feel good. And it only takes a few seconds!

Get in a Bubble

If you are stressed, overwhelmed or just tired, take a little break in a bubble…an imaginary bubble, that is. Have you experienced the feeling when you just wanted to run away from everything (especially if your work environment is stressful)? When you feel that way and don't have a chance to escape physically, use something to run away mentally.

Do this exercise somewhere where you won't be disturbed by anyone. Hopefully, you have privacy at your desk, such as in an office or a cubicle where you can relax when you want. If you work in the open environment where privacy is hard to achieve, find a place where you can relax. Is there a conference room or vacant office you can use to take a break or maybe a quiet corner in the warehouse? If every attempt fails, then find refuge in the restroom!

ACTIVITY: Place both palms side by side on your face, like you did when you played peek-a-boo when you were little. Put your elbows on the desk or on your knees so you can hold your head. Close your eyes, relax your face and all of your body muscles. Imagine yourself being in a bubble as big as three to four feet around you. Imagine settling yourself into that bubble where nobody can get to you. Feel safe, leave all of your worries outside of that bubble, and relax. Give yourself a few minutes. Escape as often as you need to!

The first time I got "in the bubble" everybody knew about it. By the time I was done and went for some water to the break room, coworkers were staring at me as I was wearing an elf costume. They thought I was having a nervous breakdown. Somebody mumbled, "Are you ok?" Needless to say, I started laughing after realizing what had just happened! After a few explanations and recommendations, I witnessed some fellow coworkers taking a break "in a bubble."

Exercise in the Morning

It is not a secret that exercising is good for you, no matter what time of the day you do it. Exercising can actually improve a few things: make you healthier, boost your confidence, and take care of the stress that you endure during the day. Some recent studies show that if you exercise the first thing in the morning on an empty stomach, you will burn 20% more body fat during the day. Increasing your metabolism is always a good thing, but it can make you feel better!

Many times we think "Oh, need to go work out later today." But when we get home, we are tired and don't have energy to do anything! So if you exercise in the morning, the rest of your day will be on a positive note, since you have that task checked off. You will feel so good to start the day with a major accomplishment that any task, later on, will look like a piece of cake! After you exercise your self-confidence is high. You deserve a pat on the shoulder – not everyone can do this!

ACTIVITY: If you can't just jump in your car and go to the gym, do some exercises that don't require equipment. You can run outside, run inside, do Zumba, salsa dance, do sit-ups and so on. And it doesn't have to be something very hard. A simple walk can be a great start to a beautiful day. If you have a dog that you need to walk every morning, then you have already done your part. Just do something! Find your perfect routine.

I had a friend who would wake up early to get her family ready for school. She claimed she had no time for exercise. My recommendation to her was to lift weights very slowly for 10 to 15 minutes in the morning few times a week. That didn't take much time for her and gave great results! Not only had her health improved, but her self-image as well. She became more confident, calm and assertive. Good for her!

Do Nothing
In today's fast-paced environment, driven by time and immediate satisfaction, doing nothing can be a luxury. The best way to relax and de-stress is to stop what you are doing and just do nothing. This can be the easiest thing for you to do or the hardest thing ever. I understand you if you suddenly feel guilty by it. We are so accustomed to rushing all the time that we don't appreciate the moment of now.

ACTIVITY: Take your time to do nothing, just breathe. Stop working, stop messaging, stop checking your email, checking your phone, stop talking, stop thinking. Be silent. Be still for at least 10 seconds, forget everything you are doing and just relax. Concentrate your thoughts on NOW. Don't think about the future, don't think about the past, but only now. Just stop.

The world will not collapse if you are taking a break. But you can collapse if you don't take a break. It is not hard physically to stop doing something, but it can be mentally challenging to stop thinking. Stop all physically activity, close your eyes, and then count to ten very slowly, while you are breathing in and out. Or you can keep eyes open and stare at something without thinking about it. Don't analyze it or judge it. Just be.

I used to feel guilty to take just a minute for myself to relax. More than that, doing nothing felt like treason. It felt wrong because I grew up in a society where only losers did nothing. I didn't want to be seen as lazy. I felt like I had to be in continuous movement. But never taking a break worked to my disadvantage. So take a break and do nothing. Put this book down. Stop reading and take a break!

10 FOODS THAT NATURALLY REDUCE STRESS

Many of us handle food differently while we are stressed. Some of us can't take a bite; when others can't close the refrigerator or pantry door. Some foods can be beneficial to our well-being and can help us to relax.

Now you are probably thinking about comfort foods and drinks such as a glass of wine, ice cream, or pizza. Unfortunately, according to Shape magazine, there are four foods that can causes stress: caffeine, alcohol, light-sodium food and saturated sugars. These foods not only cause you stress, but also increase the possibility of becoming diabetic, developing cardiovascular disease, obesity and so on.

Below is the list of foods that came to my attention as something that not only nurture your body, but also calm your nerves. By all means, I am not suggesting that these are the only foods that can improve your well-being! These are my top favorites. 1 am not a doctor. You should pay attention to your allergies and level of health in general. In addition, it is important to eat a nutritious breakfast, lunch, and dinner, healthy snacks during the day and drink plenty of water.

Dark Chocolate

I am starting with chocolate because I LOVE IT! And as Audrey Hepburn said, "Let's face it, a nice creamy chocolate cake does a lot for a lot of people; it does for me." And it does for me too. And there have been times when I have eaten a whole chocolate bar all by myself.

When you eat dark chocolate, it regulates levels of the stress hormone cortisol and stabilizes your metabolism. Quality dark chocolate is rich in Iron, Fiber, Manganese, Magnesium, Copper, and a few other minerals. Chocolate has a wide variety of powerful antioxidants that protect cells from free radicals and causes a notable decline in blood pressure and heart disease. Cocoa also can improve brain function. What can be more relaxing than having a little bit of sweet cocoa on a lunch break?

But the secret is – don't eat too much of it! Chocolate bars usually have so much sugar and other ingredients you don't need. The recommended amount per day is only one square or substitute with chocolate that has no sugar or preservatives. I will share a healthy and delicious alternative to eating chocolate bars and puddings. I can guarantee – you will wonder how something so easy can be so delicious! So keep on reading!

Avocado

Did you know that "ahuacate," a fruit prized among the Aztecs since way before 500 B.C. finally arrived in the United States in 1915? It was hard for Americans to pronounce, and some were calling them "alligator pears." And in the end it was named by farmers as "avocados." I had no idea that "ahuacate" is the Aztec word for testicle, named for its shape and was believed to be an aphrodisiac.

But that is not the reason I am recommending you eating this amazing fruit. And again – avocados have great health benefits and benefits for stress. They are rich in B vitamins monounsaturated fats and potassium which fights stress, anxiety and helps to lower blood pressure. Avocados are also rich in glutathione, and that is a substance that blocks intestinal absorption of bad fats that cause inflammatory bowel disease.

Avocados contain more folate than any other fruit and more potassium than bananas. After guavas, dried apricots, and dates, avocados are the highest among fruits in protein. Avocados also contain lutein, lots of vitamin E, beta-carotene, and other vitamins. Avocados supports healthy blood pressure levels, lowers the risk of macular degeneration, and even cataracts. It can also significantly reduce symptoms of osteoarthritis.

Peel an avocado like a banana – don't use a spoon because then you leave a lot of the best nutrients, which are found near the skin. Did you know that the avocado seed holds many nutrients? Don't throw it away! I grind avocado seeds in a food processor and add to my smoothies and salads. If you are not in love with avocado now, wait until I share my desert recipe!

Honey
Honey is very healthy and nutritious. It has been collected by humans for thousands of years. Besides being a natural skin moisturizer and antibiotic, honey also reduces inflammation in the whole body, including the brain. It also fights depression and anxiety. Honey can boost memory and helps with calcium absorption.

Honey possesses antibacterial and antifungal properties. It is also used to treat dandruff and seborrheic dermatitis (both caused by an overgrowth of fungus). Add honey to warm water and wash your hair to maintain a healthy scalp. If you are not using honey in your daily life, I recommend using it as a substitute for sugar. Some people say that honey is not that healthy, but you can make that choice for yourself. Personally, I love honey and use it when I can.

Are you ready for my favorite no-guilt dessert that you will love? Well, if you love avocados, that is! It is incredibly easy. This dessert requires only three ingredients: ripe avocados, raw unsweetened cocoa powder, and honey. The measurements will depend on how many and how big the avocados you want to use. Start with mixing the avocados in a blender, then gradually add cocoa and last add honey to taste. After all is mixed, the consistency should look like pudding. If not, you are welcome to add milk or a splash of olive oil. I usually add almond milk. Enjoy!

Banana
I was surprised to find out that bananas do not grow on a banana tree! They are not actually trees. Bananas grow on the tallest perennial herb in the world. Bananas have been a snack food for a very long time due to high levels of vitamins and minerals.

A medium banana has as little as 100 calories, 3 grams of fiber, 27 mg of magnesium, vitamin C, and other minerals! It is full of potassium that is crucial for proper nerve and muscle function as well as for keeping a healthy balance of fluids in the body. Due to tryptophan, which the body converts to serotonin, the mood-elevating brain neurotransmitter, bananas help with fighting stress and elevating the mood. Bananas also good for bone health and metabolism, weight loss and so much more! Eat bananas as a healthy snack between meals or after a workout to replenish your energy levels.

I used to place all my fruits in one big bowl for everyone to eat in the kitchen. Green bananas would ripen too soon to be eaten later on and the majority of them I would use for fruit leathers. Only then I found out that ethylene, a chemical from apples (both in the same fruit bowl) would ripen bananas faster! So if you want to ripen your green banana faster – put them in a paper bag with a ripening apple or tomato.

Green tea

Legend has it that a famous Chinese emperor, Shen Nung, (2727 B.C.) was sitting in his garden enjoying a cup of warm water. Suddenly, the wind blew a leaf into his cup from a nearby tree. Soon the water turned a golden yellow color spreading a strong refreshing scent. Since then green tea, and tea, in general, are enjoyed as a refreshing drink all around the world.

Green tea is a plentiful source of L-Theanine, a chemical that helps relieve anger. Green tea also burns fat, improves brain function, protects against cancer, improves dental health, and so much more! For maximum benefits drink 4-5 cups per day. Other teas that are good for relaxation are chamomile, lemon balm, lemon grass or verbena.

I didn't like green tea at first, to be honest with you. It was bitter, every time I would make it. And then I found out how to fix the taste. So if your green tea is bitter, use whole, loose-leaf tea, not the bagged type. Pour hot water, but not boiling, let it breathe for 3 minutes, then pour into the cup. Now, I no longer use boiling water for green tea, steep only for one minute, and I love it!

Oatmeal

I am sure you have heard that oats are healthy for you. Oats were used for many centuries to feed the livestock. Oats were cultivated in China as early as 7,000 B.C. but the Greeks were the first people who made porridge from oats. Many countries eat oats as a breakfast or as an additive to the main dish.

Oats reduce blood pressure, cholesterol, protects against cancer, and also enhance your immune response to diseases. But did you know that this complex carbohydrate contributes to your happiness by causing your brain to produce serotonin? Serotonin is a feel-good chemical that creates a soothing feeling, helps overcome stress, and improves sleep.

I recommend eating organic, all natural rolled oats for easy and fast cooking. I don't recommend eating instant oats since those are full of sugar, preservatives and other ingredients that can be harmful to you. If you don't eat cereal for breakfast that includes oats, have on hand some low sugar oatmeal cookies for a snack during the day. You can enjoy a healthy oats cereal bar to boost your energy level right before you finish work. It will keep you energized, balanced, and calm on the way home.

Berries
The majority of berries are a nutritional powerhouse. Ancient Romans used strawberries as a remedy for bad breath, gout, fever, sore throat, fainting, and depression. All kinds of berries, including strawberries, blueberries, raspberries, and blackberries, are rich in vitamin C, which combats stress, lowers blood pressure, and lowers cortisol levels. Berries also help to keep mental sharpness, control weight, and diabetes.

Eat berries with your cereal for breakfast, add them to smoothies or just snack on them during the day. I recommend using fresh berries or frozen berries. I also recommend eating organic berries, since nonorganic berries are saturated with toxic pesticides that are harmful to you. Don't count jams as a healthy snack since they are loaded with harmful sugar. Avoid eating toast with peanut butter and jam. That will do more harm than good.

I love eating berries with yogurt, oats, and honey as a dessert after a meal or as a healthy snack that I eat in the late afternoon to keep my energy balanced.

Mango
If someone gives you mango, consider that as a sign of friendship. At least that is what it means in India when someone gives you a mango. According to Hindu mythology, the Sun Princess was burnt to ashes by an evil sorceress. From those ashes grew the mango tree. Mango flowers were so fragrant that an emperor fell in love with the tree. When the ripened mango fell to the ground, it turned into a beautiful princess. Of course, the emperor married the princess, and they lived happily ever after.

The mango is highly respected among many cultures; it is the king of fruits. And no wonder why. I recommend eating this fruit because it is packed with a linalool that helps lower stress levels. It also protects the body against colon, breast, leukemia and prostate cancers. Mangos also regulate diabetes and help with weight loss, reduce kidney stones, and are high in iron and calcium.

Eat mangos when they are fresh, if possible. Eat them raw, as with all fruits, because mangoes contain healthy nutrients when uncooked. Preferably choose organic, or you could also choose frozen mangos. Add mango to desserts and Asian inspired dishes or eat them on their own as a quick snack in the afternoon and get an energy kick to carry you throughout the rest of the work day.

Asparagus
The saying "faster than cooking asparagus" was created by Emperor Augustus and it means quick action. He loved the vegetable so much that he formed the "Asparagus Fleet" composed out of the fastest runners to transport fresh vegetable to the Alps, where it could be frozen to eat them later.

Because of the high levels of folate and vitamin B, asparagus is an excellent remedy for curing anxiety and stress. Asparagus is also a splendid source of fiber, vitamins A, C, E and K, as well as chromium, (a trace mineral that increases the ability of insulin to transport glucose from the bloodstream into cells). It helps fight certain forms of cancer, such as bone, breast, colon, larynx, and lung.

Add asparagus to your diet in your main dishes or as a side. You can also crunch on them as a snack between meals. I personally think that preparing asparagus right is an art. I am still learning to cook that perfect asparagus batch!

Cashews
The last food that I would like to mention are cashews; they are an energy and happiness powerhouse. Did you know that cashews grow on an evergreen cashew tree like a seed? Although not considered to be a nut, cashews, like nuts and seeds, should be eaten raw. Many eat roasted salty nuts thinking they are eating healthy. But the truth is seeds and nuts lose all their nutritional value during the process of roasting, leaving only sugars and bad carbohydrates that just add to our body weight.

Cashews are an especially good source of Zinc and magnesium that helps against anxiety and depression. Zinc is very powerful in the prevention of numerous cancers. Like many other healthy foods, cashews keep your heart healthy, lowers blood pressure, helps with bone strength and joint flexibility, battles migraines and certain cancers, improves memory, and protects against UV damage. To enjoy the enzymes and the all other goodies contained in seeds and nuts, we need to soak cashews in water for an hour or more before eating.

Since our bodies have no way of storing Zinc, it's important to get some every day. Snack on them between meals to keep your energy elevated. Just make sure don't eat more than a hand full at a time.

COWORKERS

We spend more time with our coworkers than with our families. As you can see, it can be very stressful to deal with coworkers, especially since you don't have the freedom to talk to them or correct their behavior like you would with a family member. Stressful relationships with coworkers are a big reason why people quit their jobs. Even a mean boss or low salary is more tolerable than stressful coworkers.

The University of Tel Aviv conducted a study over 20 years and came to the conclusion that employees who did not have "peer social support" were 2.4 times more likely to die than those who had successful workplace relationships.

If you manage your business from home, you probably think that this topic doesn't apply to you. But once in a while, you may meet a fellow human who can make or break your day, so keep reading. For everyone else who does work in a fully packed of coworkers environment, you can learn a few tricks. Below are a few of my strategies for dealing with annoying coworkers, and even how to stand up for yourself and build honest, productive relationships.

Listen to People

Everyone wants to be heard. In today's social media society everyone is talking about themselves. They take pictures of the food they eat, share with everyone that they are in a bad mood, or post pictures of every little thing their pet did. Many just talk about themselves.

Be different. Listen. Just listen to someone talk. Ask others a few questions; How are they doing? What are their plans for the weekend? You would be surprised how big of an impact you will make to a person if you just let them talk. Of course, consider your schedule and how long they talk, because conversation should not stress you out. Give them space to talk, keep eye contact, nod your head, listen to them and mean it.

One of my clients served his company as a senior manager. After working for this company for over thirty years, he decided to retire. In his honor, coworkers organized a party in an expensive restaurant next door. He liked the dinner and the attention. But the most of all, he was impressed with a young employee who asked many questions about my client and was sincerely listening. My client told me that "Instead of everyone trying to impress me with their achievements and pushing me for endorsements, this young fella was genuinely interested in me and my experience. That attention itself made my day."

Build a Rapport

We all depend on relationships with other people. Many people behave differently at work than when in their personal surroundings with their family and friends. Many coworkers are enjoyable and funny. And if you don't get to know them, then you will never know that they are fun. Well, you can say that there is no need for you to know if they are funny or interesting. But I am sure you would like to have a coworker who you can trust or turn to when you need to ask a favor.

Ask your coworkers about their weekend. Ask them how their family is doing. If they went on a trip, ask them how it went when they come back. If they were sick, ask them how they feel. Show interest in them. When you get to know them, you will understand them better. More than that, when you show interest in them, they know they are noticed. And everybody wants to be acknowledged and appreciated for who they are.

If you have a chance, invite your coworkers for lunch outside of work, or eat with them in the break room during work hours. If you have time after work, invite them for a drink. Chat about the latest news or shows you love. Ask them about their kids, grandchildren or pets. These are favorite conversations amongst people. Also, don't forget to share things about yourself; don't be secretive and untouchable.

I have had many coworkers who were very friendly and caring people. They were very approachable, helpful, and trustworthy. They were like family to me. People like that made my life easier at work. Wouldn't that be nice if you were surrounded by people like that? Start with yourself! And you can be somebody like that to others.

Have Manners
You can thrive in life if you just be nice and ask for what you want. So many wonderful friendships and partnerships are being forged because people are nice to each other. Always treat others as you want to be treated. Show respect to others, and they will show respect to you.

Don't talk in a demeaning voice or talk down to people or treat them as they are incapable of doing something, or stupid, or incompetent. Some people you work with maybe not be as experienced as you are. And that is okay. But it is not okay to put them down or to gossip to others about them in disgust. Respect them for who they are.

Be polite and say "Thank You" when somebody helps you, and say:" Bless You," when someone sneezes. Say "Good Morning" when you come to work and "Have a Good Night" when you leave. Small things like that don't take much time to do, but it makes a huge difference in building relationships. When you are nice to people, people are nice to you.

I had a supervisor that would come to work and would not even make a sound. I never heard from her a "Good Morning" or "Thank You." She didn't think that talking down to people or rolling her eyes at someone was bad practice. Maybe she was displaying her power that way, but she surely built a lot of resentment in our team. And when she asked us to come in to work extra hours to increase her group sales quota for the year, nobody signed up. She was not nice to us, so we were not nice to her. Don't let this happen to you.

Be Respectful
Nobody likes to be talked down to, spoken to in a raised voice, to be laughed at, or to be made fun of. I am sure you don't like it when you are treated in those ways, so treat your coworkers as you would want them to treat you. The workplace is the wrong environment to take your steam out if you are not happy.

It doesn't matter if you think you are right about something or if you are the boss and believe that showing power somehow should influence people around you positively. The truth is, the more you disrespect people, the worse the relationships will be, and productivity levels will drop. Treat your coworkers and team with respect, even if there is someone in the crowd that you think is not worthy of your respect. You are better than that, so keep your standards high. And respect everyone, not just those that you like. If you are disrespecting some coworkers, but are nice with the others, anyone who sees your behavior will disrespect you, not only the person that you are disrespectful to.

So watch your tone of voice and body gestures. I had a client who was complaining that his team wasn't productive enough and he would have low productivity levels. I asked him to describe his day in detail. And that is how I find out that he had made negative remarks to some of his employees about the other employees. He would complain about how someone is lazy or someone is stupid. He would make ironic remarks to his employees and thought they were "funny." My recommendation to him was to show more appreciation and respect towards others and talk positively about others. It took a while to rebuild respect from his employees, but he did it, and his firm became successful as he wished for.

Be Open-minded
It is a good idea to be an open-minded person. It helps to understand others by seeing where the other person is coming from. We all are different, and have different points of view. This is not necessarily a bad thing. Of course, I am not talking about dangerous extremes, but for moderate differences, I invite you to open your mind to your fellow coworkers who have a different background and may see things differently.

I believe we are stronger when we think differently and when we are open to other people's opinions. It helps us to see things outside the box. Everyone can contribute to the project you are working on. More than that, if you will open your mind and give a chance for somebody else to deliver a new point of view to the conversation, you can learn not just something new, but also bond with your follow coworkers. Everyone wants to be noticed, acknowledged, and appreciated. Taking note and listening to other points of view is very empowering.

If you think you are judgmental of other's opinions and actions, next time a coworker talks or makes a decision that you don't agree with, ask yourself what was the reason for that. Imagine yourself in your coworker's shoes. What would you do? Being open minded, you also need to be compassionate and understanding.

I had a friend who loved her work and she was good at it. Since the time she was a child, she was very independent, and rarely asked anybody else for help. At work, she would rely on her opinion only. Not because she thought that her opinion was the best, but because she felt that the employer was paying her for her expertise, not for someone else's ideas. One day she ran into an issue that she thought had no solution. My recommendation to her was to talk with her coworkers and ask what they thought. And by listening to others and by opening her mind to other perspectives, she found the perfect solution and achieved great results. So don't be afraid to open your mind and think out of the box.

See Greatness in Others
Wouldn't it be nice if you received acknowledgment for all of your great work? To be recognized for the putting forth your best efforts and for helping others? If your coworkers and supervisors already see greatness in you, then you are one of the luckiest ones. Many employees lack acknowledgment and appreciation from the people they work with. Many employees would rather take a lower paying job where they are appreciated than a higher paying job, but be ignored despite their efforts.

When I had full-time jobs, there was a pattern to the cycle of my experience. At the beginning of my employment I would be very inspired to do my best at the workplace. I would be on time, I would work extra hours without pay, I would go to work sick to make sure the job was done, and jumped in to help others the first chance I got, and so on. As my employment progressed, I noticed that nobody acknowledged my hard work and sacrifices. My supervisors would even expect me to do more without "Thank You," "Great Job," or a pat on the shoulder. Soon, my passion and drive faded away, and I would move on to a new job.

We all need recognition and appreciation; that is just being human. Your coworkers need the same from you. So when somebody does an excellent job – thank them! When someone goes out of their way to perform well, reward that effort. When somebody makes sacrifices, acknowledge them. It is that simple. And it doesn't have to be monetary. A positive word, a pat on the shoulder, a thank you note can go a long way. And when you appreciate others, others will appreciate you.

Change Your Point of View
If you have a coworker that annoys you a lot because they keep on demanding unreasonable things from you, change your perspective. Try to see things from their point of view. Better yet, ask them why they want what they want. Many people do things differently than others, and if you can see their point of view, you will understand them better. You probably will have more empathy for their demanding behavior if you know why they obsess about the details in the report. They don't want to look unprepared or sloppy in front of their boss. Everyone has a reason why they behave the way they behave. Find out what it is.

Sometimes, people demand things without an end. Nothing's right for them. It is like they are irritated that you can't read their minds! In that case, the reason for such a behavior is personal and has nothing to do with you. They just take out their agitation on you. They are probably upset at somebody else in their lives or even themselves. Have compassion for people like that because they could be very lonely or going through a difficult time.

One of my clients had a supervisor that was impossible to work with. The older lady was very picky and had unreasonable demands for simple things that can be done with ease. She would work long hours and would complain about her lack of sleep. My recommendation to her was to change her point of view and try to understand why her boss was so overwhelmed. More than that, I recommended being personal with her. One day my client complimented her boss, and asked how she was doing working such long hours. After her boss had felt the sympathy, she became more reasonable.

Share Credit
Have you ever had a brilliant idea at work and shared it with a coworker? Or have you helped a coworker to solve an issue with a project, only later to find out that he presented your idea to the management as his own without mentioning your name? I am sure that made you feel angry. You wished he would have given you credit!

The same goes the other way. If you are working on a project, and a coworker helped you, mention him or her by name at the meeting, or include their name in the report. Acknowledge and appreciate others for their ideas, help, and contributions no matter how small. This type of behavior will build trust between you and your coworkers.

I had a boss once that was the best boss I ever worked for. He would always mention everyone who helped him with a project, report or a meeting. He would even thank and mention our office assistant by name, claiming that if not for her great morning coffee, there would be no satisfactory and fruitful meeting! Needless to say, everybody loved him.

Be Calm
It is not a secret that calm people win more than those who raise their voices. I understand, sometimes it is impossible to keep your cool. It's

understandable if you are a football coach and yelling is the only way you communicate with your team that are out on the field. But in most circumstances, flaring out and losing your temper on someone is not the way to achieve your goals.

If you want to get your message across, keep your voice down. Being calm works not only with coworkers but with friends, spouses, and children. It is the person who is calm even in the middle of the storm who is seen as a leader, as somebody who is in control, someone people can trust, respect and go to for help. Be that person. When you think you are losing your cool, just breathe in few times and ask yourself will raising your voice to get you the results you want. Just imagine what will happen if you lose your temper. You don't want to act foolish, so keep your voice down. If you can't talk calmly, don't talk at all. Approach the issue later or in writing, it is hard to scream in a letter.

One of my friends had a boss who would raise his voice any occasion he found. Everyone in the office would stress about it. My recommendation to my friend was to keep calm when his boss was having a temper tantrum. After few tries, seeing that my friend was calm and not giving in to panic, the boss would calm down more quickly, or would not make a stressful attack at all. And soon my friend was actually promoted! I am sure his calm behavior contributed to that.

Don't Assume
I don't think there is a workplace where everyone is happy, polite and calm. It is just impossible to find a perfect workplace. We are all human and bring our worries with us to work. Knowing this, if someone is rude to you, don't judge them right away. I understand that it will be hard to hold back, because from your point of view you are being attacked. Your best response is to keep yourself safe and instead of being angry, be curious.

You have no idea why that person was rude to you. I don't believe there is anyone on the planet that would like to be rude just for the fun of it. If someone is, they are acting from a place of hurt and pain. No happy person would hurt another person in any way. So if your coworker is rude to you, try to understand them and try to find the cause of why things are not going well between you two. You can ask them in a calm tone of voice if you can help them. Maybe there is something that they don't want to cooperate about with you on a shared project and by clarifying the issue, you can mend that connection. Try to figure out the reason or what is triggering the behavior. You will be surprised to find out that it is not you—it's them!

Once I had a supervisor who would be mean to people around him in general. He would come in to work already in a negative mood, be upset about something a secretary didn't do, complain about low sales, and get onto somebody for no reason. We all thought he was very mean, and that is a nice way of putting it. Only later, we found out that things at home had not been going well. His only son was very ill, and my boss had no control over it. He felt powerless and like a failure. That is why he would get out his frustrations on his employees. So if someone is rude to you, don't judge them. But if you feel bad, don't be rude to others.

Stop the Bullying
It is hard to believe that bullying still happens in the work environment. But it doesn't mean that you need to suffer, even if your boss or supervisor is the bully. First, start with acknowledging to yourself that you are being bullied. It has happened to all of us, so there is nothing to be ashamed of here. And truly, being bullied has nothing to do with you, and it is instead the other person's problem. The bully influences your day negatively only if you let them. So after identifying that you work with a bully, set the limits. Think of what you would like to tell that bully and how you would like to behave towards him

or her. The best way to handle this is not to be intimidated or scared, and when you don't act that way, a lot of times the bully backs down. Know your worth. Stand up for yourself. Show your strength.

If ignoring them or standing up to them doesn't work, then you need to address the issue. First, talk with the person you have a problem with. Many times I have seen that the bully has problems of their own and takes out their pressure on others. Some have issues with personal traumas in their lives and can't imagine that they are hurting other people. Talk to the bully and tell them how you feel. Remind them that it is important to stay professional in the workplace. If the bullying still continues after you talk to them, talk to your supervisor or involve management if you have to. But there is no reason you should put up with that kind of behavior, even if you are afraid of losing your job. Many times, the bully attacks not only you but others. By speaking up, you will be protecting somebody else, too.

I had a client who would get bullied by her boss. She was afraid to say anything to others since the bully was her superior. After she started talking about her issue with coworkers, she found out that there were others in the workplace that suffered bullying from the same boss. They all made a decision to go to the boss as a group and express their concerns. Since the group made 1/3 of the whole office, the boss took that intervention to heart and improved his behavior.

Don't Point Fingers
We are social creatures. Many of us work in groups. Some thrive in the group environment; others prefer to work alone. But I am sure you will agree with me, that it is impossible to get along with everybody. Perhaps it's not you that keeps the distance, but not all coworkers like to be a part of the group. Some teams work together better than others. But no matter how close the group is, or how well everyone knows and understands each other, there will be times that somebody will point the finger at someone else. That is the way things are

in a group. Humans are addicted to righteousness. Everyone wants to be right and better than the other. Competition may move things forward, but pointing fingers at each other may stall any progress altogether.

So before you complain about your coworker, look in the mirror. Examine yourself first. Have you ever made mistakes? Maybe you've come in late? Maybe you were on the phone too long? And maybe you are an excellent employee and have compassion for others. Many things that may be noticing and judging others for are small and irrelevant to your life. So let it go!

I had a coworker who lived to gossip about who was late or who didn't do a good job. I kept on telling her that she didn't know all the details of their lives, so how could she judge them. Pretty much all of us are doing the best job we can at a given moment; try to be on time, and follow the rules. Not everyone gets the same set of circumstances, and it all depends on how we react to those circumstances. A few months later, she was late to work a few times because her car broke down, her kids hid her car keys, and she over slept. After that, she stopped judging people who were late, gained a new compassion and understanding that some things are out of your control and there may not be much you can do about them.

Don't Blame
Whatever we do, we always do the best we can in a given situation. Working with others involves cooperation and trust that the other person will give the best too. Some people perform better than others. Some people have more knowledge, experience, and tenacity to ensure projects are accomplished. But it doesn't mean that the other person is not doing the best they can.

When working in a team, or even in a partnership, it is easy to point fingers at one another and blame the other person for poor overall results, or for mistakes that occurred while working on the project. Never play the blame game. If you blame others for errors and poor performance, you will be blamed too. And what does that say about your character if you blame others? Have compassion for others. If you see that the quality of work is not up to par, offer your assistance to your coworker. And if mistakes happen, find out why, and try to prevent them next time. Remember, you are all in this together. There may be a time in the future when your coworker will help you out!

I had a coworker who blamed her assistant for deliverables not being on time. Although her assistant worked long hours, my coworker thought that her work quality was not up to par. One day, in a meeting, my coworker noticed that the report title was misspelled. She accused her assistant of letting a mistake like that slide, and only later she found out that the title was correct, and my coworker had been misspelling it all through the report. Her assistant could have just let it be printed incorrectly and blamed my coworker, but instead she corrected it in silence.

More Than Words
Since childhood, as people we learn to read others body and language and feelings behind their words in order to survive. By now in adulthood we all know that the actual words we say are only the part of the story. How we communicate with coworkers can make or break the relationship. Communication is key not only between coworkers but also between other people in our lives: friends, family, and acquaintances. So it is important that your communication is flawless, or else you may get yourself into trouble!

Actual words are about 10% of all communication. The rest of it includes your voice and body language. It is important to pay attention to your voice and make sure it doesn't sound offending. A good way to communicate with the other people is to keep your voice calm and quiet. No matter what you are communicating to your coworker, you need to speak with respect.

There are numerous studies about body language and how it affects our communication. It's a good idea to talk to your boss by standing up straight, it shows your confidence. And it's not a good idea to talk to somebody with your arms crossed as that position shows defensiveness. Facial expressions and your eye movements are also a very important part of communication. A single glance can stop your coworker in his tracks. Rolling your eyes, when somebody speaks to you, is considered vulgar.

I had a client who wasn't happy with the relationship with his employees. I asked him how often he talks to them. After hearing his habits of being bossy through his posture and tone of voice, I realized that even a simple adjustment could improve his work relationships. My recommendation to him was to talk with his employees softly and calmly, to initiate meetings by sitting with everyone at the same table, and to watch his habit of crossing his arms on his chest, which symbolizes opposition. It was hard to change his habits, but in a few months, he reported much warmer relationships with his employees.

Clarify Your Intentions
Everyone has different perspectives and ways to do things. And there are no bad ways to do things, just different ways. So if you ask somebody to do things your way instead of theirs, you should clarify to them what the value is in following your approach. Without explanation, some of your coworkers may see you as just being difficult. By explaining your logic to them, you help them see your point of view. That way you won't appear so bossy.

A good leader is one who inspires others to follow them, and not the one who gives orders to follow. You may be thinking that leadership is not your thing, and you are not planning on being a leader anytime soon. But even then, a simple task that you are asking your coworker to help you with will be executed much faster, and they may be more willing to see your point of why you are doing it when you act like a good leader. Better yet, when you are asking for help, ask what your coworkers think of the task and give them a chance to lead. Consider that somebody else may have a better idea of how to do things! Maybe somebody has already done this task and can share their experience. When you involve others with your task, suddenly you are on the same level together, and you are not bossy or difficult.

I had a supervisor once, who was very bossy and wouldn't explain things. He never cared if his ideas are valid and demanded to meet without argument or doubt. He wasn't a team player, and by no means was he a good leader. After he had left the workplace, many confessed that he was the worst boss they ever had.

Express Emotions
We all have emotions. Some of us show how we feel more than others. I think it is healthy to express your emotions and show the others that you have a heart. Someone can argue that not all workplaces are appropriate for showing emotions, but I disagree with that idea. Even the strictest work environment can benefit from expressing appreciation, joy, and enthusiasm.

Expressing your emotions to your coworkers is healthy. It shows that you are honest with them, you trust them and you feel comfortable with them. At the same time, your coworkers will feel the same about you. Of course, not every emotion you have should be shared. It is a good idea to show joy, appreciation, excitement, positivity, and support. It's a great idea to show sadness or disappointment, but it should be accompanied with the understanding that your emotions may influence other people. So before expressing negative emotions, think of how they could impact others.

I had a friend who would complain that every job she had, she could never find a connection with her coworkers. She felt as if she was very different than them, making her feel lonely and like an outsider. I asked her what the other coworkers were like, and she described that many of them would have lunch together, laugh together and so on. But nobody would invite her to join them for lunch or talk to her. I asked her to talk about herself to her coworkers, show her emotions when she was happy about something or sad. I also recommended that she react to other's emotions and be supportive. And as soon she showed her emotional side, her coworkers started to respond to her, and she felt like a part of the group.

Apologize
Take responsibility for your actions and any mistakes you have made. If you see that you hurt somebody's feelings, apologize. If you have done something that you didn't mean to do on purpose, apologize. If you made a mistake because you didn't know, apologize. And I hope you won't do things on purpose to sabotage somebody or hurt somebody, so you don't need to apologize for that.

Depending on your personality, an apology can be a very hard thing to make. And that difficulty doesn't mean you are weak or need approval. It shows the strength of your character. Not everyone can acknowledge their mistakes and make things right with another person. Just ask yourself: do I want to be right, or to be happy? An apology will take the weight off of your shoulders. When you apologize to another person, it shows that you are open, you are honest, transparent, and trustworthy. And that works not just in the relationships with your coworkers, but also with your family and friends. When you are open to people, people will open to you.

I had a client who was so sure about his righteousness; he wouldn't even apologize when he was late to his session. His relationships with his family and coworkers were deteriorating. In his mind, an apology meant weakness and he was afraid to look weak. My recommendation to him was to list all of his conflicts or issues that he was having with his wife and chose at least one issue that he knows he did wrong. His homework for that week was to apologize to his wife for what he had done. The next week I saw a different man. Apologizing to his wife solved a lot of hurt feelings they had for each other and it finally gave them space to breathe. I am sure the flowers he bought for his wife just made things better. I think that was the first time I saw him smile!

Have the Last Word
It is a good idea to be the last one who ends the conversation. It has nothing to do with acting superior over somebody. I mean something different – leaving a conversation on a positive note. To make a positive impression doesn't cost a dime, and it doesn't take much time. When you are leaving your workplace, make sure you say "Bye" to everybody that you meet on the way out. If you have a conversation with somebody that helped you, make sure to thank them. If you helped somebody and they thanked you, reply with "You are welcome" or "With pleasure."

Some conversations should end in a positive way, especially those that have a negative undertone. There is a way to cut a conversation short without being rude. You can be nice, save your time and still get a positive vibe. If you have a coworker who brags all the time, it is a good idea to interrupt the conversation with a positive "Wow, I am so happy for you." and go on with your day. If there is somebody who keeps telling you what you need to do even if you didn't ask them, thank them for their help.

Have an Escape Plan
Once in a while you will come across coworkers who just don't seem to understand that you value your time, especially in a workplace. Some people love talking so much, that if you let them, they can bother

you all day! Every workplace has them. And they are friendly people, but sometimes they prevent you from doing your work. If you have a coworker that keep on coming to your workspace and keep on interrupting you, you need a plan. If you don't want to offend his or her feelings, you can use a few simple techniques to save yourself from hours of gossip, complaints, or flattery. There is no need to be rude to them or disrespectful. Figure out the best ways you can escape those coworkers.

You can use these simple ways to remove yourself from your workspace so they can't find you. If you see them approaching from afar, grab a piece of paper and go somewhere else. Act as if you are busy at the moment. If the coworker approaches you and asks something, just answer "Did you see Mary today? I have a question for her." And keep on going. Make a circle and come back to your place. I am sure that annoying coworker will have replaced you with another victim. If somebody gets to your place and you have no chance of picking the phone or acting like you are busy, then just stand up and go to the restroom or to the printer. I am sure they won't follow you! Keep on escaping them until they stop coming.

One of my friends had a coworker that would sit in her cubicle and chew his tobacco for hours. Annoyed and disgusted by his habit, she tried leaving him behind her cubicle. Unfortunately, he would be waiting for her! So she had an understanding coworker next door who would save her in those situations. So when the tobacco king came to her cubicle, the coworker next door would call my friend on the phone. She would pretend that she was talking with her boss. She would open up some document and would start explaining what she done. After few minutes, the tobacco king would leave. If he stayed, she would pretend that her boss asked her to stop by his office. So she would apologize and leave. Everyone knows that taking with the boss can take a while, so the annoying coworker would leave her alone.

5 Steps How to Deal With Negative People

We live in a world with such a diversity of human character. There will always be people with negative attitudes towards everything. No matter how good or how bad things get, they are always complaining - for hours. You can't change them. So how can you try to keep yourself sane when they around?

1. First of all, identify who are the negative people in your work environment. When someone complains to you about how bad it is, determine if they are they just venting because they had a bad day and they may need to talk to someone. But, if they keep venting to your day in and day out, every day over time, then they may just be negative. And you can expand this idea and apply it in more areas than just the workplace. A negative person can be even a family member! It can be your boss, the coworker who works right beside you, or someone who comes for a visit once in a while.

Now you know who they are. The best defense is to ignore them as much as you can. Stay away from them as far as you can. Don't go to them to talk, don't contact them in any way, unless, it is entirely necessary. For example, the negative coworker that sits next to you will be hard to avoid, but you can stop swinging by to check on someone if they make you feel bad. Sometimes it is impossible to avoid these kinds of people. If that happens to be a coworker that sits next to you, a neighbor that keeps on popping in uninvited, or a friend who calls just to complain, or other people that you just can't get rid of, you have to accept the unfortunate situation and learn how to deal with them.

2. No matter who the difficult people are in your workplace, don't take their behavior personally, even if the most annoying person is your boss or your supervisor. I understand, you may think you have to depend on their moods since your paycheck is dear to you. But their inner turmoil is truly not your business.

Don't take their words or behavior as a deliberate attack towards you. How coworkers act has nothing to do with you. It is all about them! We are all obsessed with ourselves, thinking about ourselves all day—good and bad—and since they are not thinking of you all day, don't think of them either. Your coworker's everyday dramas are more important to them than you. They think of their dramas; they react to them, and they behave as if they believe that the drama fits them. You are only as small part in their lives. Stay out of their negativity and don't let it change your day.

Same works for you. Others can't rock your boat if you don't let them. So it is better for you not to take things personally or you will end up being offended for no reason. There is no need to defend your values, beliefs, or to get involved in their drama. That involvement will just escalate the conflict.

3. When you encounter a negative person, before you act on your feelings, stop. Just stop and take slow deep breaths. Concentrate on your breathing. Of course, there is no need to exaggerate these movements so the other person notices, just take subtle slow breaths. Remember that no matter what the other person is telling you, your primary goal is to keep calm no matter what. Don't get sucked into the negative mood of that person. Observe yourself and the other person objectively. When you are able to observe the situation with objectivity and not emotion, you can free yourself from the negative emotions the other person is expressing.

As much as possible, always practice defenselessness with negative people. This doesn't mean that you don't care about them, or you let them guide your values, but it places you in a position where you don't spend energy fighting against them. Be as neutral as possible with what they are saying. Just let them express themselves. After you can calmly hear what the other person is saying, express kindness and compassion to that person. You don't know what happened to them that day. There is a reason why they are acting the way they are acting. Your compassion towards them will keep your spirits up and won't let you sink into their negative hole. Maybe the other person just needs to talk with someone. Maybe they are going through something hard in their lives and just need an ear to listen to them a little bit. Being compassionate is a trait of a strong person.

Just remember, you have been happy and sad at some point in your life, so you know how it feels. You probably experienced in your life sickness and misfortune the same as the other person. And always remember the person in front of you is doing the best they can in a given situation. They are not trying to hurt you on purpose. They are asking for help. And if you can remember that, no matter how difficult the person is in front of you, you will approach him or her with a positive attitude which will help the other person to feel more positive as well.

4. If you don't like the person that is in front of you, don't let it show! No matter how annoyed you are with him or her, don't frown or roll your eyes at them. No matter how irrelevant the matter they are talking about or stupid it might sound, don't start talking down to them or raise your voice when you are responding. Be respectful to yourself and with your fellow coworker. You are more than that. Don't tune them out or ignore them altogether. That usually doesn't help either. If they want to talk, they will just talk louder and louder so you have to pay attention to them. The best practice – just listen to them! And don't just listen to them and say nothing. They will think that you don't understand them, and will repeat the story or tell you in more detail.

And remember, if you disagree with something they say, but are afraid to tell them you disagree, you are silently agreeing with what they are stating. It is important to differentiate yourself so the negative person and anybody around you won't think that you agree with the negative views. You want to be sure to draw the line and get as little involved as possible. You may feel compelled to agree with them on the poor-me trip, but you need to understand that the more you pity them, more they will continue talking. It is good idea also to restrain from sharing any personal stories sharing because this is not productive work time. I am sure you don't want to your boss to see you as an unproductive employee – even if you are talking with the boss herself!

5. If a coworker complains to you about something, offer your help. You might even think that they don't need help or maybe you can't even help them. The only way to find that out is to ask them! And it can take such a simple thing to get the complainer to stop, just ask him, or her if they need help. There will be some things you probably won't be able to deal with, but many times people don't even know what help you can offer. Some things can be very easy to help with; some might need a manager's assistance.

If your coworker accepts your help, give your advice and your opinion freely. After all, they asked for help, so why keep the solution all to yourself? Don't be afraid to tell the truth, and don't be afraid to offend the other person. You might be inspiring her for something new or may give a totally different point of view of the situation that probably she didn't think of! Hearing a different opinion is always helpful. When you give advice do not talk down to the person or ridicule them. If someone is approaching the problem in different way than you, it doesn't mean they are less than you. Help them with respect.

So give you opinion and see what happens. If the person still continues to argue with you about why your suggestions won't work for them, advise that they contacting their supervisor. And if you spend plenty of time opening their eyes, showing them a different point of view and coming up with multiple solutions, but they won't take any of your suggestions, then it is time to end the conversation. You have already spent too much time on them, and if they think nothing will help them, then you definitely won't help them either.

Some people love to complain and have deep beliefs of victimhood. That is something they need to work on, it has nothing to do with you. Just let them be. They are choosing the life they want, so don't get offended if they don't follow your advice. Wish them well and let them go. End the conversation by telling them that you need to go back to work, after all, you are all here to do your jobs. Or tell them you need to use the restroom, make a phone call, or go to the meeting.

Don't spend too much time on concentrating on negative people. Above all your focus should be on how much stress you can endure from difficult situations with your coworkers. To function well, you need to be at peace with yourself and with others. Don't get involved in drama, gossip or any other activity that doesn't make you feel good. Spare your mind from negativity. Keep your stress levels as low as possible! You are in control.

How to Have a Difficult Conversation
It is not easy to have a difficult conversation. The difficulty can be a touchy subject, important news, or a person that is hard to communicate with. No matter what, there are steps that will help you to keep the conversation comfortable and as stress-less as possible. When it's time for the difficult discussion, be confident and assertive. For example, you if want to address the issue that your partner is not cleaning the dishes.

1. Find out the truth, do some investigation of the facts. Be clear about what is wrong. No matter how painful the facts are, look them in the eye. Write down your facts the way you see them and ask yourself

if they are true facts. Think of times that your partner cleaned the dishes and when they didn't.

2. When you are done with evaluating the situation, contemplate and decide on what outcome you want to have happen. Not knowing how you want things to change will make the problem even worse. Write them down what you are expecting out of the conversation and how you want to see the problem resolved. In the case of cleaning the dishes, I am sure you want them to be cleaned right away.

3. When you are ready to talk, start the conversation with something positive. If you are afraid you will hurt somebody's feelings, it can be scary. Start with a compliment, flattery, and acknowledge something that the person is doing well. That will give a positive note and improve the success of the conversation. Explain your reason for the conversation. Explain to them that you are willing to talk about it to make things better because you care for them. Say that you loved it when they cleaned the dishes after the family dinner last week and is not that they are not doing it at all, but you would appreciate more help.

4. If you are talking about the behavior that you want to address in the other person, don't accuse the person of being bad. Point out the behavior that is causing the trouble. Separate those two, because the same person has other behavior traits that are positive. Don't say that they are too lazy to wash the dishes. Point out the actual dirty dishes that you are upset about.

5. When addressing the issue, try to present as many details as possible. Don't tell them in generic terms, such as "You don't care about me!" Give them a specific example "After I come back from work, there is so much to do, and the dirty dishes just make me feel unappreciated by you. You can help me more around the house."

6. Remind them, again, with details, about the time that they did something good. Give them another example of things that they handle well. That will take away the impression that you are attacking them. So no need to be defensive about the problem, and then the conversation should flow peacefully. Tell them that you appreciate their cooking, fixing things, taking care of the kids, or whatever they do well.

7. After you stated the issue, tell them what you want the outcome to be. Tell them to help you, change their habits, take care of you more, and clean the dishes and so on. Clarity is very important, or the other person will be hopeless with vague ideas. Say "I would love it if you take care of the dishes more for me. That will help me a lot!"

8. After you stated you case with details, in a calm voice and coming in peace, you should ask what the other person thinks of the issue. Ask them how they see the issue and what they are willing to do about it in the future. Don't hesitate to ask the person "What do you think about that?" and wait for the answer. After you hear the answer, do something to change the situation!

MANAGING YOUR TIME

Time is a very precious thing. As I say, the time is flying by, the next thing you know, it's time…well, let's just say, it is time to retire. We all get 24 hours in a day. Then we are suppose to sleep for eight hours, so that leaves us with 16 hours to do what we please. Or can we truly do what we want?

If you are preoccupied with things that you should do, and most of the time you do things for somebody else, then you probably have no time left for yourself. That is the problem I mentioned about Mary at the introduction of this book.

As Brian Tracy says in *The Law of Planning*: "Every minute you spend in planning, saves 10 minutes in execution." I think that idea the key to making every day be a productive day. And with a little time management, you can accomplish more than you think.

Below you will find great time management tips and tricks that helped me and my clients to squeeze the most out of 24 hour a day, move mountains, and still stay energized by the end of the day.

Prioritize

I recommend you to start your day with a to-do list. Managing tasks can be very stressful if you are not sure what your goals are for that day. If you don't have a list to go by, here is what I learned from Brian Tracy.

1. As soon you get to your workspace, write down all the things you need to do. Even things that are not due until next week or even next month. Write that down on a piece of paper or type it in a word document on a computer, whatever makes you feel more comfortable.

2. After you are done, you will make a simple to-do list into a priority list. Without a priority list, you won't be clear on what projects are due when and when they need to be completed first.

3. Now, read your list one by one and rate it by importance. Write a letter "A" next to a task that needs to be done today. Something that needs to be done tomorrow rate it as "B." For tasks that can wait until next month or when you have time, rate as a "C." After you're rating is done, start tackling your list starting with the "A's" work at it until they are all done. When you're done with the "A's" proceed to the "B's" and then the "C's."

When you start to implement this system, it will get easier every day, because you will have a starting list from yesterday to begin your new day. I can't even function right if I don't have a prioritized to-do list. I make a list even for the weekend, for vacation and for anything I can. I just love crossing off my daily load one by one until it is all gone! Then I reward myself for a job well done.

Plan Your Day Ahead of Time

If you have a to-do list, and I highly recommend that you do, then planning your day ahead is much easier. And you will eliminate even more stress if you plan your tomorrow the night before. That way you know what your tomorrow will look like and there will be no surprises. At least you will be prepared for events you know.

Make your list of things to do the night before. If you don't want to make a list or there are only a few things that you will remember, it is alright just to think of them.

I usually think of tomorrow's tasks right before I go to sleep. After I have figured of all the accomplishments, victories and completed tasks and goals for that day, I think of my new tasks that await tomorrow. This process gives me peace of mind so I can sleep with a smile.

Use a Calendar
It can become very stressful to manage events that you are not prepared to handle. Some events happen in our lives in a way that we can't predict, such as a car accident. But predicting when the bills are due, when your next meeting, or when a report is due, those are easy to predict and manage.

Use the organizer to keep up with to-do lists, projects, upcoming events and other miscellaneous items. Write everything, no matter how small it is. You think you will remember your friend's birthday, but you won't. Not being organized is truly not an excuse. And just having a calendar won't help you if you don't use it. To see results, you need to use it!

Set yourself reminders for projects that you need to complete, so the deadlines don't creep up on you. Break a project into a doable schedule and put it on your calendar so that you can keep yourself on track. With today's technology it is hard to escape all of the calendars and reminders. There are plenty of programs and apps that can sync your calendar to your phone and keep you updated by reminder alerts or emails.

I had a client who had so many calendars and to-do lists simultaneously, that he got lost amongst them. He would misplace an ongoing to-do list and then start a new one every few days. Many things got forgotten because he didn't centralize all of his goals. I recommended having one master calendar and sticking to it.

Time Your Activities
It seems that there is too much work to do during the day. Some activities are important, such as eating, sleeping, going to work, taking care of the family and so on. But some activities are not so important, but we still do them to relax and entertain ourselves. And that is a great way to fight stress. Taking breaks during a busy day, is necessary to keep living healthy. Unfortunately, if someone doesn't know how to manage their time during the day, juggling all these activities can become very stressful.

Some activities take all of our time, and they shouldn't. Many activities we do can be done later or on a different day or delegated to somebody else. It is important to identify how long you spend on different activities and then give them a time limit so that you can keep up with other tasks. Use a timer to remind yourself when to stop with one activity and proceed to the other. Don't forget to give yourself a buffer for the transition to go from one activity to the other.

I had a client who claimed to have too much to do and not enough time to do it all. She was taking care of her four children and running a successful yoga practice. Many of her activities couldn't be accomplished in the same day, and they had to be done periodically, such as working out, leading yoga classes, picking up her children from school. Her stress level dropped when I recommended to her to group the activities together and set a specific time to do them. A few events were scheduled to be performed less often, and many relaxations or entertainment activities were cut in half. After making a few changes to the schedule, she felt more in control and more relaxed.

Intend To Be Early
Being so busy does not make it easy to manage arriving to all of our scheduled activities on time. For most events and activities, they have a starting time. In the society that I live, I am being expected to arrive on time – not even few minutes late. If you belong to the society where being late is not a big deal, you are already saving yourself from a great amount of stress.

Managing all your daily duties and being on time while you are fighting the traffic is very stressful. And maybe you don't have to travel to a different location, but maybe you need to finish a project, or prepare for a presentation. No matter if you are going to work, to an appointment, or submitting a project, plan to be early.

So leave earlier! When you target to be on time, you end up being there on time or late, depending on traffic and you are probably stressed about being late. Even if you are great with planning ahead, there could be something on the way that becomes an obstacle to your well-polished plan. But if you intend to be there early, you can give yourself extra time to get there, so you arrive relaxed and on time.

I learned that one the hard way. I used to be late. I tried very hard to be well prepared and leave the house on time. But then something would come up on the road. At some point, I decided to pretend that my appointment was not at 3:00pm, but at 2:45pm. This one thing changed my stress levels! If something came up on the road, I wouldn't be stressed because I knew, in reality, I still wasn't late. If there was no traffic on the road and I would arrive early, my appointment would be happily surprised, and the meeting would go much more smoothly because they see my commitment, I am a trustworthy person.

Learn to Say "No"
We all have busy schedules, deadlines to meet, goals to accomplish and we must take care of those that we love. Trying to please everyone can get very stressful, especially when you don't have time for it.

If your day is full already, pace yourself by remembering your priorities. There will be a time when you need to say "No" to additional obligations expected by your friends, family members, neighbors, and coworkers. I understand. It is hard to tell other people "No" when they rely on your friendship. It is very hard to tell them that you can't help them. But it is worse to promise you will do something, and then don't deliver because you are overwhelmed with other things you already promised. Pace yourself and know your limits.

I had a client who would agree to do everything that her family asked her to do. At some point, she was spending all her of after work hours caring for her aging mother and two siblings. She felt obligated to take care of them. After a while, she felt guilty for not spending enough time with her family. Only after learning to tell them "No" to obligations she couldn't fulfill, she found peace and stability in her life.

Delegate
It can become very stressful if you have to do everything by yourself. More responsible jobs require more work and accountability. I recommend balancing your workload with your capabilities by delegating tasks to others when you can.

Let's face it – it is hard to do it all by yourself, It is also hard to trust others to do what you expect them to do. And there is always the possibility that you won't get the results you expect. But you need to keep the faith that all will turn out well. Always inspire another person for better results, be appreciative and thank them for a job well done. Delegating is not only good for decreasing your workload, but also increasing the success on a common project. It is just impossible to be the best at everything! You are good at some things, and somebody else is good at other things. Why not use them for the common good?

I had a client who was a team leader and felt responsible to do many things by himself in order to look good in front of his management. More than that, he felt that his team was taking advantage of his hard work and they were not doing much for themselves. The reality was simple: he didn't trust anybody with his work. After he took my recommendation to delegate some of his tasks to other team members, he found that their relationship improved and became more trustworthy. After he had given them a chance to show what they were capable of, he didn't feel resentful towards them anymore.

Single Task
With so much to do during a work day, it makes sense to multi-task. After all, women are notorious for multi-tasking. I remember a picture of a mother who is cooking dinner with one hand, holding a child with the other and is talking on the phone at the same time. This topic is so important that it is in the first chapter of this book, and I include it here as well because it applies to both sections. So, if you missed it the first time, here's your second chance to start single-tasking.

Depending on activities you do, and how important they are, you can multi-task. But if you are working on a serious issue or on a project that requires attention to detail and high responsibility, I recommend single tasking. When you do an activity, concentrate only on that. Don't try to do many things at the same time, the quality of your work will decrease, and you will be left with mistakes that need to be corrected later. Save yourself from the headache – concentrate only on one task at a time!

Do everything in your power to be less distracted. Some things in your work environment you have no control over, but many you do. Turn off your cell phone, close out extra tabs on your computer, don't work on multiple projects at the same time and don't chat with coworkers or a friend while you work.

I had a coworker who would work on a report and message coworkers at the same time. She made a lot of mistakes and received a lot of negative remarks from her supervisor. Only after she turned off every distraction, she finally could manage to concentrate and improve her work quality.

Keep Small Stuff Small
We have a tendency to stress ourselves out even if there shouldn't be a reason for stress. We over-think and overdo many times. We worry what others think of us; we stress at how we look in front of others, and we hassle to perform a job perfectly. You have to learn to let the small stuff go. Many things are not that important and won't make a difference in your life in the long run. If you are unsatisfied with something, ask yourself "Will this be important ten years from now?" If no – let it go!

Here is the simple reality: no matter how hard you will try to make everything perfect; the truth is that you never will. There be always somebody that won't be happy with what you have done, or how you looked, or what you said. And there will probably be things that others won't do the way you want them to be done for you, they won't look good enough, or they won't do what you asked them to do. So what? Stressing over these things don't help you – they just harm you. It is time to let that go.

I have a friend who used to worry too much about the small stuff; she would give herself anxiety by over thinking and analyzing what her coworkers thought of her and what they meant by what they said.

The more she paid attention to those things, more things to worry about showed up in her mind. I recommended that she ask herself if those coworkers were so important in her life that she should spend so much energy on them. I invited her to ask herself if they will be at her bedside in her dying hour. And if no, they wouldn't, so why worry so much about them?

Cut Short Long Conversations When You Need To
In today's world so many people are afraid of offending the others. Out of respect we will hear someone out when it is not convenient for us. But if you are in a hurry and the other person won't stop talking, it can be stressful. I recommend cutting conversations short.

Don't be afraid to share that you have somewhere else to go or something else to do. Cut the meeting or conversation off when it goes beyond the time you can spare. Some meetings last way too long, and some of the time is spent on unimportant conversation. The same goes with personal conversations. Cut the meeting short when it reaches the nonproductive line. Don't be afraid to do that. That way you will save the rest of the day being on track not just for you, but for others too.

I observed one of my coworkers for the longest time being very chatty every time someone came to her cubicle. At the same time, she wasn't doing her work the way she should be; she made a lot of mistakes and her supervisor was not happy. When she complained to me about it, I recommended that she stop chatting for so long or while she was working. She explained to me that she felt obligated to talk with people and she needed to do her job, so she did both at the same time. After a short conversation with her, I noticed that she stopped talking and working at the same time and had the courage to tell her coworkers "Ok, I am going back to work now." Her quality of work increased, she exceeded her supervisor's expectations for the quarter and soon she was the employee of the month.

LOVE YOUR WORKSPACE

I want you to think of your workspace. Or even look around if you happen to be there. Is it neat and clean? Is it easy to find anything that you can think of'? According to OrganizedWorlds.com the average office employees spends about 1.5 hours or 6 weeks per year just looking for things.

The Neat as a Pin white paper "The price of disorganization in the workplace" by Jennifer Snyder CPO states that "Time spent searching for misplaced items in the office combined with searching for lost files on the computer; the estimated annual dollars spent reaches more than $177 billion annually."

These are scary numbers. Are you one of those people who stresses over things that you can't find in your work environment? Let's take care of it! Below you will find great advice on how to organize your workspace and keep your sanity. Don't be intimidated by the long list. After it all is done, you will be very happy you did the tasks.

Clean Your Workspace
Over time there are so many things that can accumulate in our workspace. And it doesn't matter how big or small the workspace is, somehow we manage to overload it with stuff that we think we will need.

Humans are funny beings - they like gathering stuff. Many workspaces are full of things that are old, not useful anymore, or just plain useless.

One way to cut stress and relax your mind is to clean your workspace. Just not seeing old things around will put your brain at ease. No matter where you work, in an office, in a cubicle, at your desk, or at your workspace, it needs to be clear. Even a space with only counter can still be cleaned. Even if you are a driver and have no desk or counter, your car is still your workspace. It should be free of clutter. Identify items in your workspace that you don't use anymore and throw them away. Get rid of everything that you don't need or want. If there are things that you think somebody else can use it – give it away.

One of my clients complained that her office was too small to organize anything; she had piles of old paperwork everywhere. I recommended that she scan and make digital copies of the important information, and then shred all of it. After she was done, she was so surprised to see that her office was quite big!

Gather and Put It Back in its Place
Has this ever happened to you: you are in need of a stapler, reaching out to the place where it should be, and it is not there! You look everywhere and you still can't find it. It could be anything like a file, a book, keys or anything that is movable. It is very stressful when you try to find something in a hurry and it's not there where it should be. Does this problem seem familiar? Is your workspace organized? Can you imagine a workspace where everything has its place and it is always there? Imagine someone asking you where the stapler is and you can tell them without looking "on the top shelve next to the red box."

One way to get rid of this stress is to get things in order. Gather up every item that is in the wrong place, not where it belongs, and put it where it should be. If you decide that something fits better in another place, change it. But everything should have its own place. Get in the habit of putting items back where you got them, so you don't waste time finding them in the future.

A friend of mine had very unorganized office. Once she had a client who was about to sign a long term contract with the company she worked for. My friend was looking for a pen, and couldn't find it. And more she was looking through her paperwork, drawers, and even in her purse, the more her client became uncomfortable. After an intense search, finally, the client stood up from her chair and left her office without signing the contract. If she had been more organized, she wouldn't have lost that client.

Label Things
Not all things in your workspace can be put in plain view. Label boxes, holders, shelves, bags, bins, baskets, drawers and anything else that need a label. Labels are great reminders where the things should go. That way when you use them, it is easier to put them back where they belong. That way you don't stress to find your things!

Pick labels are clear to read, serve the purpose, and appeal to you. Labels can be in all different shapes and colors to differentiate themselves between the things that are stored. You can buy them or you can even make them yourself.

I had a coworker who loved arts and crafts. Everything in her cubicle was organized, and every little thing was put into a proper box and labeled. Next to the label she would even make a drawing to represent what was in the box. Her labels were so ornamental, original, and unique that other coworkers asked her to make labels for them. Soon she was making labels for household items. Last time I heard, she quit her job and was making labels for sale.

CRUSH STRESS WHILE YOU WORK

Improve Your Filing System
Having boxes and holders in your workspace to organize paperwork is a good thing. Although, the files can cause stress when those holders are full of old, useless paper, and it is hard to find the right piece of paper because the pile should have been stored in some other way.

To reduce stress when you are looking for the right piece of paper, go through your existing holders and clean them up. Keep paper documents only if you truly need them, for example, an invoice that you need to send back would be important. If you have different types of paperwork that needs to be stored, create more folders to store them, place them in a drawer or a box. Paperwork that is already old or has served its purpose can be stored digitally in your office. For digital documents create a filing system on your hardware. If you are already storing data on your computer – clean that up too. Go through those folders and see what documents can be deleted to free up some hardware space. Back-up your data systematically.

I had a client who was working for a big company responsible for invoicing. Every day she would receive and send many bills, some in the mail, and some digitally from her email. Some invoices were paid right away, some later, and some were overdue. It was a very stressful situation since she needed to keep up with so many things all at once. After determining the priority order, we came up with a very organized filing system that involved as many folders as needed to work efficiently and my client had a system that kept her well organized and sane.

Clear Off Your Desk
It is hard to concentrate and perform your work when your workspace is cluttered and unorganized. It can be very stressful and overwhelming if you don't have enough space to work. If your workspace is small you already have a space challenge. But if your workspace was

big enough to function correctly, but you created so much clutter on it, then you can change that.

Something as simple as clearing off the clutter can already give you peace of mind. Remove all items from your desk, counter or wherever you work. Dust off, clean, sweep, vacuum the workspace itself. You want to start clean and clear. I recommend cleaning, sweeping and dusting your workspace every week. Then put back only the items that you need for everyday work. Use desktop organizers, boxes, folders, or containers to organize the items on your desk. You can use trays for paper, and small containers and boxes for small items. The leftovers can be given to somebody who is in need or thrown away. Every day before you finish your work, file any paperwork away, and put back the things you used. Try to clean your workspace so next day you come to work you can start organized, clear, and with peace of mind.

When I used to work in the corporate world, I was so tired at the end of the day that I would leave my desk a mess so I just could go home sooner. So the next morning I would face the things that I left unorganized on my desk. And no matter how good my mood was, the mess on my desk would bring me down as soon I walked into my office. So at the end of the day, I would clear my desk before I went home. My mood and productivity escalated just because I had a clear and organized desk to start my day off fresh every morning.

Organize Your Drawers
After you have cleaned your desk, it is time to clean and organize your drawers! Drawers are easy to miss as they are usually closed and nobody can see what's inside. Drawers also hide all the stuff that we don't want to deal with. That is why places like this should be organized periodically.

Take out everything that is in your drawers and filing cabinets. Make three piles: needed items, items you might need, and not needed items. Items that you need can be organized into boxes, trays, bags, shelves and so on. For items that you think you may need, imagine not having them. Take each item one by one and determine how your work day will look like if you didn't have that item. If you decide that you will need the item, then put it away. If your work day can survive without it, put that item into a third pile. The third pile with things you don't need can be given away to someone who needs it, donated to charity or thrown away if it is useless. Your goal is to put as many items you can go into your drawers to clear desk space. Also, organize them into boxes and folders and store them inside the drawers.

I used to have a coworker who everyone called the "black hole" because she would borrow things and they would never be returned to their owner. After she had left for another job, all of the stuff was discovered in her overloaded drawers: 4 staplers, three hole-punchers, three scissors and so many more things that should have been only a quantity of one each. Because she was so unorganized and dropped everything in her drawers, she never would find anything.

Sort Mail
Remember that pile of mail that you think you will get to it when you have time? Now is the time. I am sure it is stressful just to think of going through it but do it as soon as possible. It is more stressful looking at that pile every day. Just get over it. You will be proud when you are done.

1. Shred all the mail that is not necessary or past due and doesn't need your attention. I don't recommend leaving anything to read for later because most likely "later" will never happen.

2. And going forward, here is the secret of never going through the huge pile of mail again – take care of it as it comes. As soon new mail comes in, read it and decide what you will do with it; act on it or give it to somebody else. The best practice is to act on it right away,

so you don't need to do it later. After you are done with it, shred it or throw it away.

3. Don't like dealing with mail at all? Unsubscribe from anything that you can read online. Make all of your bills paperless. If you have companies sending you invoices by mail, ask then to send to you by email.

I remember myself having a huge pile of mail. I always thought that I would get to it later, but I never did! Magazines, coupons, brochures just piled up with the rest of mail, and they never got opened. If you don't read something within three days of receiving, the probability that you ever will is very slim.

Assign Discard Dates
Even if you organize your mail, invoices, and other paperwork, clutter could still pile up. And even very organized clutter still causes stress.

Many think that all paperwork is a "must" to keep until the end of days. But in reality, there is no need for you to keep every piece of paper indefinitely. Find out what documents need to be kept and for how long, and then discard them. Doing so will free up not just space, but also give you peace of mind!

If you store documents and other paper work digitally, there is the time when they no longer useful as well. If you are planning on collecting something for very long time, make sure you label folders by subject, year and month. So just in case you decide to discard them, it will be easy to know what should be thrown away first. In order to discard documents on time, set up reminders for yourself of what paperwork needs to be taken care of when.

Bring Furniture to Work
If you have a workspace, you probably spend a lot of time there during the day. Even if you work from home, your home office is a workspace.

Organized and cozy workspaces will give you energy throughout the day, help you to be more relaxed, and less stressed. Of course, if you do something that you just love doing it, then your workspace won't feel limiting to you. But even then, it should feel cozy and inviting.

Since we spend so much time in our offices, cubicles, workstations, and counters, making that area loving, inviting, and relaxing is very important. Adding simple things that you can bring from your house, such as a lamp, a rug or a plant will make you feel at home. Personalize your workspace if you can. I don't recommend you to bring half of your house and make it cluttered, but a few attributes will brighten your day.

One of my coworkers had an office that looked like a living room. She had plenty of pictures of her family and friends on the walls, multiple plants and flowers to take care of, an expensive rug, pillows on the chairs in front of her desk, plenty of small ceramic figures and an expensive lamp. It might sound a little over the top, and plenty of people in the office thought so. But I tell you this, when someone went to her office; they didn't want to leave. They felt relaxed as if they were visiting a friend. I am not recommending you to go all out if you don't want to, but you sure should make your workspace comfortable and relaxing.

Keep Yourself Inspired
With so much going in our lives and around the world every day it is very easy to get overwhelmed, stressed and discouraged. It is very critical to keep your spirits up - no matter what.

First of all, keep clear from anything that will bring you down, or make you sad or make you doubt your strength. Create defense systems that you can fall back on at any moment you feel discouraged, oppressed, or left out. Are there any inspirational quotes that you love? Place those quotes somewhere where you can see them, where you can read them when you have a free second. Sign up for a daily uplifting quote of the day. Read it and reflect on it. Place pictures of your family and friends on your desk. Keep them where you can glance at them easily during the day. Is there a destination that you want to travel to? Place an image of it where you can see it.

I had a client that felt resentful towards her work and intimidated by her coworkers. I recommended to her to bring a few things to work that gave her comfort. She brought one of her favorite cactus, a lovely picture with her group of friends laughing, a small cute, colorful rug from Turkey where she traveled last summer, and a lamp from a local antique market where she loved to browse. She created a cocoon in her cubicle where she felt supported by the memories of the things and people that mattered to her. She found shelter in her workspace where she could relax, concentrate and perform her work at her best.

ABOUT THE AUTHOR

Lolita Scesnaviciute Guarin is an active Certified Stress Management Coach and Certified Life Coach, speaker, webinar and workshop facilitator. Lolita now does what she loves and lives with her beautiful family in Houston, TX. She is dedicated to educating everyone how to manage their stress and live fulfilling happy life.

To get great stress management tips from Lolita Scesnaviciute Guarin, become a fan on Facebook at www.facebook.com/BeAmazingYou, Twitter BeBtYou, and Instagram @lolita_guarin.

To register for "Kick Stress in the Butt" consultation, go to www.BeAmazingYou.com

Made in the USA
Lexington, KY
16 December 2018